Footprint

Cardiff

Rebecca Ford

& South Wales

Contents

322632

Listings

About the author

A graduate of St Andrews University, Rebecca Ford worked in public relations and advertising for several years before becoming a full-time travel writer and photographer. Her travels now take her all over the world, although she specializes in writing about the British Isles and Italy. Her work has appeared in newspapers such as *The Guardian*, the *Daily Express* and *Scotland on Sunday*. She also writes and contributes to many other guidebooks.

Acknowledgements

Rebecca would like to thank Nerys Lloyd-Pierce, Debbie Roberts, Rachael Norris, CADW and Glenda Lloyd Davies and all at the Welsh Tourist Board. Thanks also to all the other people in Wales who offered advice, insider tips and even cups of tea.

The most striking thing about Cardiff is its energy. This is Europe's youngest capital and it bubbles with optimism. Elegant arcades teem with shoppers, tables from busy bars and cafés spill on to the streets and glistening structures of glass and steel rise phoenix-like from the former docks.

Although Cardiff has ancient origins, its past is just that – past. Its historic castle asserts no brooding presence but sits meekly on low ground, upstaged by the Millennium Stadium. The most distinctive buildings are 19th-century – a legacy of the lucrative trade in coal or 'black diamonds'. There is the Washington-white Civic Centre in Cathays Park; the glass-domed labyrinth of Victorian shopping arcades; and the exuberant red Pierhead building in the Bay.

When coal slumped, the city's spark went out. But the recent arrival of the Welsh assembly and the rebirth of the docklands, have given it a new sense of purpose. Cardiff has no weighty history to hold it back and is keen to embrace the new. This is a city that is reinventing itself – and thoroughly enjoying it too.

Black gold of the Valleys

Cardiff's wealth flowed down from the Valleys, the coal-rich regions to the north. People worked in grindingly awful conditions to hack nuggets of black gold from the earth, while the notorious slums of Tiger Bay grew up around the city's docks. The demise of the mining industry hit Cardiff hard, but it was worse in the Valleys where communities shrivelled from the blight of unemployment. Today Cardiff's dockland slums have gone, but life in the Valleys is still hard. The mountains of slag are gone, the Valleys are green, but unemployment remains depressingly high. Yet the people are warm and welcoming, and somehow these Valleys have a soul that the seat of power lacks, a soul that sings of Wales.

Cymru's cappuccino capital

Cardiff has only been capital of Wales since 1955 – and many felt that other places laid greater claim to the honour. There is no doubt that the city is not particularly Welsh. The language, for example, the thread that helps to bind a nation, is little heard on the streets: it's more widely spoken in neighbouring Swansea. And Cardiff was no ancient seat of government: it developed, in essence, as the personal coal-port of the Scottish Marquesses of Bute – a grimy but lucrative business that attracted settlers from all over Britain and across the world. Yet it was certainly the city that had the capital and it has grown into its role. Many young people now feel it's cool to speak Welsh; it boasts the country's finest sporting stadium; and is home to the new Welsh Assembly. It's the liveliest, most cosmopolitan, most fashion-conscious place in Wales. And though it's filled with bars and cafés where well-heeled punters sip cappuccino and cocktails, on international match days its streets still flow with a crimson tide of rugby-shirted supporters, singing their hearts out for their country.

At a glance

There are two parts to Cardiff: the commercial centre, which is bounded by the River Taff on the west, and the redeveloped docklands area of Cardiff Bay a mile to the south.

City centre

The Taff river flows along the western side of the city centre. Close by is Cardiff Castle which stands on the site of the original fort built by the Romans and is now, thanks to the riotously eccentric interiors commissioned by the third Marquess of Bute, one of the city's main visitor attractions. The two are separated by the green parklands of Bute Park. Also on the Taff, just a short walk from the castle, is the new Millennium Stadium, a huge 72,500 seater arena that is the home of Wales' national sport – rugby. West of the Taff, close to the city centre, is the increasingly exclusive Pontcanna district. It's an area that is popular with the Welsh media mafia – the *Taffia* as they're jokingly known – and some state that people would 'sell their livers' to buy a house here.

The northern part of the centre is focused on Cathays Park, an area that is dominated by the impressively serious and slightly sterile Civic Centre. This cluster of buildings made of white Portland stone is grouped around the Welsh National War Memorial and was built at the turn of the 20th century, a time when the city was at its most prosperous. Cardiff University, the Law Courts and the impressive City Hall (sometimes called the Welsh White House) are all here, but the main attraction for visitors is the National Museum and Gallery. This contains fascinating natural history and archaeological artefacts, and boasts fine collections of ceramics and Welsh and Impressionist art. The surrounding suburbs of Cathays and Roath are generally known as the studenty/arty districts of the city.

The railway line runs round the city's eastern side and is linked to the M4 motorway by the Newport Road. This busy artery contains a number of hotels and guest houses.

Squeezed into the compact centre of the city, in the wedge between pedestrianised Queen Street and the High Street, are Cardiff's many shops. Many are clustered into the sort of enormous modern malls that you can find in any city: Queens Arcade, the St David's Centre and the Capitol Centre all attract shoppers looking for big high street names. But there are also wonderfully atmospheric Victorian and Edwardian arcades, former alleyways that were covered with glass domes and turned into elegant shopping streets – along the same lines as London's Burlington Arcade. These arcades, such as the Royal Arcade and the Castle Arcade, are filled with specialist shops selling everything from old books to kinky boots, and bustle with locals as well as tourists. The centre is also home to St David's Hall, an unlovely building but a major venue for concerts, and a rare medieval relic – the church of St John. Many of the main bars and restaurants can be found in this central zone – to such an extent that one particularly restaurant-rich street, Mill Lane, has been renamed the Café Quarter. Even more redevelopment is planned for this central area, which will focus on the area south of the St David's Centre.

Cardiff Bay

Cardiff Bay, or just 'the Bay' as it's known locally, is the bright new face of Cardiff's docks, situated about a mile south of the centre. These were once working docks, rough, grimy, cosmopolitan and often squalid. The area was known as Tiger Bay and the slums that grew up around this salty site were notoriously tough. Now the bay has been regenerated, the focus of the controversial multi-million pound development being the creation of a marina. This was formed when a barrage was built, which allowed the flooding of extensive mudflats – once a refuge for thousands of wading birds. Now more and more new buildings are springing up amongst the remaining Victorian structures. There's the liner-like, five star, St David's Hotel;

Techniquest, a modern science centre; and Mermaid Quay which is filled with bars, restaurants and cafés. The new Welsh Assembly is now being built and the Wales Millennium Centre, which will be home to the country's National Opera, is due for completion in the autumn of 2004.

South Wales

Cardiff is a great base for exploring southern Wales. The Vale of Glamorgan to the south is little visited, but has some pleasant towns and villages. To the west is Swansea, the gateway to the lovely Gower peninsula which offers great surfing, cycling and walking just an hour or so from Cardiff. Further west is Laugharne, famous as the home of Dylan Thomas. Northwest of Cardiff is Carmarthen and its surrounding gardens, while to the north are the former coalmining Valleys and then the wild hills of the Brecon Beacons National Park, which offers a wealth of activities. Further east are the Borderlands, the brooding Black Mountains and the famous booktown of Hay-on-Wye.

Trip planner

Finding a place to stay in Cardiff when a rugby or football game is on is almost impossible, so try and book accommodation well in advance. Prices at these times will also be much higher. If you're not into sport then you're advised to avoid match days altogether. If you've come to go walking or climbing on the Brecon Beacons, then the best months are between April and October. The hills can be treacherous in winter for the inexperienced. If you're heading for the beaches of the Gower, the best surf comes up between September and April, though beginners should start on the smaller summer waves.

A day

Cardiff is a small city and the main sights are easily reached on foot. However, don't be tempted to squeeze too much culture into one day – you'll suffer overload. There are loads of options that will be partly determined by the weather, but for an enjoyable and varied day you could start with a trip to the National Museum and Art Gallery in Cathays Park, to admire the superb Davies Collection of Impressionist paintings. From there it's just a short walk back to the heart of the city for some lunch – try the contemporary Welsh food at Blas in the Old Library. Then you could treat yourself to an afternoon of retail therapy in Cardiff's elegant maze of Victorian arcades. If you start to flag there are plenty of cafés to revive you – on a fine day opt for an al-fresco latte at one of the many places that line Mill Lane, Cardiff's café quarter. Then it'll be time for an early evening drink at a traditional, your-Dad-would-love-it, Welsh pub, or a cocktail at somewhere like the trendy Sugar. After that, head off to a restaurant down in Cardiff Bay for something to eat overlooking the marina. If you've got any energy afterwards, go clubbing – Club Ifor Bach's a good choice.

A weekend

A weekend will give you time to take in a visit to Cardiff Castle as well as the Museum (or vice versa). It's the city's other main central attraction and boasts wonderfully ostentatious interiors that have to be seen to be believed. Football and rugby fans are then certain to want to take a tour round the mighty Millennium Stadium, where major national and international matches are played. Otherwise you could hop on a bus for a proper look around Cardiff Bay to see how the new Welsh Assembly building is progressing. There's plenty to see down here, including an informative exhibition on the workings of the Assembly in the lovely Victorian Pierhead Building; artworks in the Norwegian Church; and, ideal if you've got kids in tow, hands-on interactive science exhibits at Techniquest. You can also take a trip to see the engineering wizardry of the Barrage up close, or take a boat trip out to Flat Holm island.

A long weekend

Staying for a long weekend will allow you to take in some of the many attractions outside the city. On the outskirts is historic Llandaff Cathedral, as well as the excellent Museum of Welsh Life, which stretches over 44 acres of land at St Fagan's, four miles out of Cardiff. You could easily spend a whole day here poking around the cottages, farmhouses, shops and mills that were saved from destruction by being moved from other parts of Wales and painstakingly rebuilt on this site. Alternatively you could explore the little towns and villages of the Vale of Glamorgan; visit the fabulous Roman ruins at Caerleon; or hop on a train to Swansea to visit the Dylan Thomas Centre, followed by a short bus ride to adjoining Mumbles for a walk along the seafront and a deliciously indulgent ice cream at Verdi's. If you prefer more activity, then the Gower's great surfing beaches are readily accessible, with the nearest at Langland Bay, only about a mile from Mumbles.

A week

A week would allow you plenty of time to combine all the city's attractions with a leisurely exploration of the Gower, where you can breathe in the beauty of the headland at Rhossili and touch the mighty rocks of King Arthur's Stone. Or you could head north to discover the industrial heritage of the Valleys; walk on the wild hills of the Brecon Beacons National Park; or go northeast to explore the stunning borderlands, home of romantic Tintern Abbey and the famous book town Hay-on-Wye.

★ Ten of the best

1 **National Museum and Gallery** A must, even if you don't know your Monet from your Manet. The largest collection of Impressionist works outside France, p43.

2 **Museum of Welsh Life** An open-air museum filled with historic cottages, shops and mills. Best saved for a dry day, p57.

3 **Dylan Thomas Boathouse** Overlooking the silvery estuary at Laugharne, on the Carmarthenshire coast, is the inspirational home of Wales' most celebrated poet, p80.

4 **Cardiff Castle** Famed for the Marquess of Bute's gloriously flamboyant interiors, this gilded Gothic fantasy resembles a genial madman's medieval dream, p33.

5 **Cardiff Bay** Shiny 21st-century Cardiff rises from the once dingy docklands – a lovely spot for al fresco dining on a sunny summer's evening, p48.

6 **Hay-on-Wye** Bibliophiles beware, this town's one big bookshop: you won't go home without succumbing, p96.

7 **Big Pit and Blaenafon** Don't miss the chance to don a hard hat and go down a coal mine, and don't forget Blaenafon's historic ironworks, a World Heritage Site, p89.

8 **Tintern Abbey** Indulge your inner poet and soak up the atmosphere of this most romantic of ruins, p83.

9 **Brecon Beacons National Park** A visit to this huge stretch of serious wilderness is guaranteed to put roses in your cheeks, p92.

10 **Gower Peninsula** Endless blond beaches, superb surfing and megalithic monuments. Pack a picnic and come for the day, p71.

Contemporary Cardiff

Cardiff is the fishing village that became a city. And while Cymru's cosmopolitan capital has ancient origins it is not a place that is defined by history; nor is it wreathed in a murky Celtic mist of myth and legend. This is a city born of trade – a commercial city that grew rich on coal, a city that was once one of the busiest ports in the world. The legacy of this is a fresh, enthusiastic and energetic approach to life. It is easily the liveliest, most outward-looking, most European place in Wales, and one of the fastest-changing cities in Britain. This is the place to come if you want to see wonderful collections of Welsh and Impressionist art, seek out the best contemporary Welsh crafts, see a the cutting-edge band, or shop for up-to-the-minute designer clothes in some of the most stylish shopping arcades in Britain.

The capital since 1955, Cardiff has changed enormously in recent years, shaking off its stereotyped image of an industrial city with little more to offer than dodgy docklands, a rugby stadium and beer-swilling sports fans. Regeneration of the city, which had been savagely blighted by the decline of the coal trade, really began in the 1980s with the building of the St David's Centre and Hall, and the 1997 referendum in favour of a Welsh Assembly gave it increased impetus. Cardiff became the Assembly's home and began to look and feel like an international capital. Today Cardiff Bay, the redeveloped docklands area, is changing so rapidly it's hard to keep up with it. The new buildings that jostle for attention around the waterfront include a sparky new science centre and a five-star hotel and spa, which attracts a fair smattering of celebrity guests. There is also a glistening crop of bars and restaurants – all airy, light and modern with lashings of glass, blond wood and outdoor decking. Joining these soon will be the new Welsh Assembly building, on which work started in 2003, and the Wales Millennium Centre, which will be home to Welsh National Opera and is due to open in November 2004. Then, in the centre of the

New architecture for a new Wales
*The Millennium Centre will be home to the Welsh National Opera
when it opens in late 2004, giving voice to a new kind of Wales.*

city, you've got the mighty Millennium Stadium. This isn't just the
new home of Welsh rugby, it has also made Wales a top sporting
venue – the absence of a stadium at Wembley only enhancing its
reputation. Further development in the city will include a
multi-million pound international sports village that will have an
Olympic-sized swimming pool and snowdome.

A criticism often thrown at Cardiff is that it isn't particularly
Welsh. It's true that you won't hear the language spoken much on
the streets. And it is certainly an Anglicized area, feeling very
different to the rest of Wales. Perhaps that's not surprising given
the country's mountainous landscape, which means that it is easier
to reach Cardiff from London, Birmingham or Bristol than it is from
Llandudno, Caernarfon or Aberystwyth. But then this is often the
case with capital cities: Edinburgh feels a world away from the
Highlands of Scotland; Rome from Naples and the south of Italy.

Not surprisingly, given the rapidity of the changes that are taking place, Cardiff still feels as if it is trying to find its feet. The Bay still lacks character and the Assembly is much criticized. And while the chic set wearing designer labels, drinking bottled water and living in spacious Victorian splendour are here in force, not everyone lives like that. Some still prefer voluminous rugby shirts to Armani, old fashioned boozers to trendy bars – and thank goodness they do. And while there are groups of stags and hens who make it a point of honour to get legless on a Saturday night, they generally seem to be much more good humoured than their English or Scottish counterparts.

Cardiff is at the heart of a general Welsh renaissance – a so-called 'cool Cymru'. The country which was for years painted as depressing, backward-looking and wet has begun to assert itself. Images of coal-blackened valleys, chilly chapels and ladies in stovepipe hats have been replaced by sweeping sandy beaches, tanned surfers and glorious green hills. And then there are the Welsh showbiz stars who have become international names: Cardiff girl Charlotte Church, Catatonia's Cerys Mathews, Hollywood royal Catherine Zeta Jones, opera star Bryn Terfel and the Welsh speaking actor Ioan Gruffudd. The food is much more sophisticated too, with contemporary chefs using the freshest Welsh produce – not just in restaurants, but in bars, cafés and the new breed of gastro-pubs.

Cardiff's compact size makes it an ideal weekend destination and a great base from which to explore other corners of southern Wales. You can visit the castle, chill out in a café, shop till you drop, bliss out on the beach – all in a couple of days. From the city you can easily get to Swansea and Laugharne, Dylan Thomas country; go surfing on the Gower peninsula; explore the stunning Wye Valley, or visit Caerphilly's enormous castle. But despite all its attractions the best thing about Cardiff is its people. They're refreshingly cheery, friendly and helpful, and always seem willing to make time for you.

The easiest and quickest route to Cardiff and South Wales from Scotland, Ireland and Europe is by plane. There are also good flight connections from London, with a flight time of around 55 minutes. From England the cheapest way west is by coach: the London to Cardiff journey takes around three hours 25 minutes. There are fast and frequent train services from London Paddington station, as well as from Manchester, Birmingham and Bristol. Journey time from London is only two hours and to get the best deal you should book in advance.

Getting around Cardiff itself is easy. The centre is small and all the main sites can easily be explored on foot, although Cardiff Bay is about a 20-minute walk away, so you might prefer to take one of the regular buses. Exploring out of town sights is easiest if you have your own transport, though there are trains and buses from Cardiff to Swansea, Carmarthen, Merthyr Tydfil and Abergavenny. More remote parts are often only accessible by bus and it's best to plan your journey in advance, especially if travelling on a Sunday when services are limited.

Getting there

Air

The main entry point to the UK is via London's five airports. Heathrow is the largest and the busiest in the world; the other long-haul airport, Gatwick, is slightly smaller. London also has Stansted, Luton and the exclusive City Airport. There are daily direct flights to them from most provincial UK airports as well as much of Europe. Flights from North America arrive at Heathrow or Gatwick. Low-cost airlines generally fly into Gatwick, Stansted or Luton. Fares are highest from around early June to mid-September and also at Christmas and New Year. Flying on Friday or the weekend is often also more expensive. The best way to find a good deal is on the internet, see box on page 21.

There are direct flights to Cardiff from London City airport every day except Saturday, as well as regular flights from provincial UK airports, Ireland and several European centres. There are also daily flights to Amsterdam, from where it is possible to fly to airports all over the world. During the summer many charter flights swell the airport traffic with planes flying direct to popular holiday destinations in Europe as well as to Toronto. Fares are highest from around early June to mid-September, which is the tourist high season, and drop either side of the peak season – mid-September to early November and mid-April to early June. However, prices will rise in winter if a rugby game or other big sporting fixture is taking place in Cardiff. Low-cost operators offer very cheap flights, but check the hidden surcharges before booking. They are also subject to rigid restrictions and need to be booked well in advance.

From the UK and Ireland **Air Wales** fly from London City, Newcastle, Plymouth, Cork and Dublin. **BMI baby** fly from Glasgow Prestwick, Edinburgh, Belfast, Cork and Jersey and **Ryanair** fly from Dublin.

From Continental Europe **Air Wales** fly from Brussels. **BMI baby** fly from Alicante, Malaga, Palma, Paris, Prague and Toulouse. **KLM** fly from Amsterdam (AMS) from where there are three flights a day.

From Canada and North America Direct flights to Toronto may operate during the summer, otherwise journeys may be made by travelling via Amsterdam, from where there are frequent flights direct to Cardiff, with a flight time of just one hour 25 minutes.

Airport information **Cardiff International Airport** (**CWL**), Rhoose, near Barry, **T** 01446 711111, www.cial.co.uk, www.cardiffairportonline.com. Wales' small international airport is 12 miles (19 km) south west of Cardiff's city centre and around a 30 to 40-minute taxi journey. The terminal's facilities include a few small bars selling drinks, snacks and teas and coffees, newsagents, a selection of duty free shops, and a children's play area. The airport is easily reached by car via the A4055, or taking the A4225 from the A48 or junction 33 off the M4. The **taxi** office is in the arrivals hall and taxis can be prebooked on **T** 01446 710693, approximately £20-25 per journey. **Air Buses** operate between the city's Central train and main bus station and the airport every 30 minutes, approximately costing £2.90 for the 30 to 40-minute journey (operating Mon-Sat from around 0650-1800, then every 60 minutes between1936-2236. An hourly service operates on Sundays).

Heathrow (LHR), **T** 0870 0000123, www.baa.co.uk, is about 20 miles west of London on the M4, just beyond the M25. Four terminals: 1 for most domestic flights, 2 for most European flights, 3 and 4 for international. Journey time to central London by underground (the cheapest option) is about 50 minutes; by Heathrow Express train (**T** 0845 6001515) to Paddington about 15 minutes (£25 standard return). A taxi to central London will cost about £40 and take about an hour.

Airlines and travel agents

Air Wales **T** 0870 7773131, www.airwales.co.uk
BMI baby **T** 0870 2642229, www.bmibaby.com
Ryanair **T** 0871 2460000 or 0871 2460016, www.ryanair.com
KLM **T** 08705 074074, www.klm.com

Other websites

www.expedia.com
www.lastminute.com
www.opodo.com

www.travelocity.com
www.ebookers.com
www.cheapflights.com

London Gatwick (LGW), **T** 0870 0002468, www.baa.co.uk, is 30 miles southwest of London on the M23, near Crawley. Two terminals: North and South. Journey time to central London by Gatwick Express (**T** 0845 8501530) to Victoria about 30 minutes (£21.50 standard return). A taxi to central London will cost about £75.

London City (LCY), Royal Dock, **T** 020 7646 0000, www.londoncityairport.com, is 6 miles east of the City of London. There's a five-minute shuttle bus to Canning Town (£2.50) from where you can get the Jubilee Line or Docklands Light Railway into central London. A taxi to the centre will cost about £25.

London Luton (LTN), **T** 01582 405100, www.london-luton .co.uk, is about 30 miles north of central London on the A1. A coach to Victoria takes one hour 30 mins and costs £12 return. City Thameslink trains run throughout the day, cost £20.80 for a standard return and take 30 mins. A taxi to central London costs around £55.

London Stansted (STN), **T** 0870 000303, www.stansted airport.net, is also about 30 miles north of central London on the M11. Stansted Express trains to London Liverpool Street (standard return £24) depart frequently and take about 45 mins. A taxi to central London will cost around £85.

Car

The M4 crosses the Severn Estuary via the Severn Crossing toll bridge (£4.50 per car, toll payable westbound only – you can leave Wales for free!). This is the main route from London and the most direct way to reach Cardiff by car from southern and western England.

Coach

The city's main bus station (T 02920 666444) is situated between Cardiff Central Railway Station and Wood Street. The bus station is served by long distance **National Express** buses (T 0870 580 8080, www.gobycoach.com). There are eight buses a day from London (Victoria coach station) to Cardiff. The journey time in total is three hours 25 minutes and a return ticket costs around £28. Buses from Glasgow take around 10 hours to reach the city, and a return costs around £63, while buses from Newcastle take around 8½ hours and cost about £62.50 return.

Ferry

Swansea-Cork Ferries (T 01792 456116, www.swanseacork ferries.com) runs both car and foot passenger services to Swansea docks from mid March to mid January. They sail four times a week – more frequently in high season. Prices cost from £22 single for foot passengers. The journey takes 10 hours.

Train

Cardiff Central Railway Station, the main railway station in Cardiff, is situated in the heart of the city, next to the bus station. **First Great Western** runs hourly services from London Paddington to Cardiff: journey time two hours. There are also three services a day from London Waterloo. A supersaver fare costs £41, though cheaper fares may be available if booked well in advance. Travel on Fridays is generally more expensive. Regional railway lines provide a direct link to Cardiff from

Travel extras

Money Cardiff needn't be an expensive city to visit. Cheap accommodation is available in hostels or B&Bs, transport is relatively cheap, and you can get by on £30-35 per day if you eat in cafés and pubs or cheap restaurants. Also, most of the museums and galleries are free. If you want to enjoy the city's better restaurants and go out at night, then you'll need at least £50-60 per day, without being extravagant.

Safety Cardiff is, in general, a reasonably safe and civilized place. Aside from the ubiquitous nuisance of drunks on public transport and around the city centre at the weekend, most visitors should encounter few problems. However, some precautions should be taken. As in all large cities, you should avoid walking alone at night in quiet unlit streets and parks. Locals advise not to walk to the Bay at night.

Telephone code Dial 02920 for Cardiff from outside the region.

Time Greenwich Mean Time (GMT) is used from late October to late March, after which the clocks go forward an hour to British Summer Time (BST). GMT is five hours ahead of US Eastern Standard Time.

Tipping Tipping is at the customer's discretion. In a restaurant you should leave a tip of 10-15% if you are satisfied with the service. If the bill already includes a service charge, you needn't add a further tip. Tipping is not normal in pubs or bars. Taxi drivers will expect a tip for longer journeys, usually of around 10%, and most hairdressers will also expect a tip. As in most other countries, porters, bellboys and waiters in more upmarket hotels rely on tips to supplement their meagre wages.

Travel essentials

Manchester and the Northwest, from Birmingham and the Midlands, and from Bristol and Plymouth. Trains from Manchester take three hours 50 minutes and cost around £40. For more information call **National Rail Enquiries**, T 08457 484950.

Eurostar operates high-speed trains through the Channel Tunnel to London Waterloo from Lille, Paris and Brussels. You can then pick up one of the three daily trains to Cardiff, or take the London Underground to Paddington.

Getting around

Further information on public transport and getting around Wales can be obtained if you contact **Traveline Cymru**, T 0870 6082608, www.traveline.org.uk.

Bus
Cardiff Bus (**Traveline Cymru**, T 0870 6082608, www.cardiffbus.com) runs services all over the city from its base in Wood Street, and its green, white and orange buses generally operate between 0530 and 2320, with a reduced service at the weekend and on public holidays. Prices vary according to the system of colour-coded fare zones, Zone A (red) is the city centre, where tickets cost from 65p. Exact change is needed and tickets may be bought on the buses.

The main routes between the city centre and the Bay area include the following: 6 Bay Xpress, www.cardiff.gov.uk/bayxpress (departing from Central Station), 35 (from Wyndham Arcade on St Mary Street to Mermaid Quay) and 8 (from Wood Street to Atlantic Wharf), and these services run every 10-15 minutes 0730-2300. A 24-hour **CityRider pass**, costing £3.30, gives you unlimited travel on all Cardiff Bus services within Cardiff and its near neighbour Penarth. This can be purchased on the buses or from the bus sales office in Wood Street.

Ancient language

Don't worry if Welsh isn't your strong point: Wales is officially bilingual and you won't find it difficult to find your way around.

Car

City-centre parking is heavily restricted and the presence of eagle-eyed traffic wardens encourages the use of the pay and display NCP car parks spread around the city centre, as well as the use of the voucher parking system. Vouchers can be bought in advance from local shops (£1 for an hour).

Taxi

Taxis can be found in the ranks at Central Station, Queen Street station and on Duke Street by the castle. A taxi from Central Station /Wood Street Bus Station to Cardiff Bay costs around £4 one way. Taxis may be hailed on the street or, alternatively, can be ordered by telephone from dozens of firms, including **Dragon Taxis** (**T** 02920 333333) and **Capitol Cars** (**T** 02920 777777).

Train

Arriva Trains Wales run most local train services (**T** 08456 061660, www.arrivatrainswales.co.uk) which run between 0500 and 2430 on weekdays, with a reduced service at weekends/ public holidays. A shuttle train service takes three minutes to run from Queen Street station in the city centre to Cardiff Bay station, from where Cardiff Bay is a five-minute walk. There are four services per hour on weekdays, two per hour on Saturdays, but no service on Sundays (from £1 off-peak). Travelling to Cardiff Bay from Central Station costs the same but takes longer, including a change at Queen Street.

Arriva also offer a Day Explorer pass for £6.50 adults, £3.25 kids, allowing for one day of unlimited travel on their train services and Stagecoach buses, as well as discounts to some tourist attractions around the city. Arriva also runs services to Swansea, Newport, Abergavenny, Trehafod in the Rhonda Valley and Merthyr Tydfil (from where there's a bus link to Brecon). To visit Hay-on-Wye you'll have to get a train to Hereford, then a bus to Hay.

Walking

It's easy to walk around the city centre, as it's small and flat – so no tiring hills. South of the centre is the revitalised docklands area of Cardiff Bay reached by the dead straight and uninspiring Lloyd George Avenue – which is fine during the day, but locals advise not to do it at night.

Tours

Boat trips

Bay Island Voyages, from Mermaid Quay, Cardiff Bay, **T** 02920 484110/01446 420692, www.bayisland.co.uk Offer high-speed boat trips out to the barrage and around the bay. A 30-minute trip costs £6 adult, £4 child. There is also a one-hour Coastal Cruise that takes you through the barrage and along the coast round Penarth and Lavernock Point, £12 adult, £6 child. They also offer one-hour 30-minute trips to Flatholm Island, which is rich in bird life, price £16 adult, £8 child, and a two-hour trip that includes both Flatholm and Steepholm Islands, price £20 adult, £10 child. There are only 12 seats on the boat so booking is required.

Cardiff Bay Cruises, from Mermaid Quay, **T** 02920 472004, www.cardiffbaycruises.com Operate half-hour cruises of the Bay on an 'African Queen' lookalike (£3 adults), and one-hour trips in the Bay, on the rivers Taff and Ely and to the Barrage, on the *Canberra Queen* former lifeboat, £6 adults.

Water Bus, Cardiff Cats, **T** 02920 488842, www.cardiffcats.com or www.cardiffwaterbus.com Run water buses between Cardiff Bay or Taffmead Embankment (approximately 300 yards from Central station in the city centre) and Penarth and the barrage. Runs daily from approximately 1040 to 1800, and on weekends and holidays in winter. Mermaid Quay or city centre to barrage goes every 40 minutes and costs £3 return, a round trip is £5.

Bus tours

City Sightseeing tour buses, Apr-Nov, **T** 02920 384291, www.city-sightseeing.com/cardiff, *£7 adult, £2.50 child, £5 student*. Open-top bus tours do a 50-minute loop from the Castle, taking in 11 stops. You may hop off at any point before joining a later tour within a 24-hour period.

Train trips

Cardiff Barrage Crossing, from Mermaid Quay, opposite Techniquest, Cardiff Bay, **T** 02920 512729, www.cardiffroadtrain .com, *1100-1700 Easter-end Oct, £3 return adult, £2 return child, £8 return family*. Family-friendly trip, with informative commentary, on a little train taking you from Mermaid Quay to the Port of Cardiff and on to the Barrage. The trip lasts just under one hour, but you can get off to see the Barrage if you wish and return later.

Walking tours

Creepy Cardiff, Ghost Tours, **T** 07980 975135, www.creepycardiff.com, *£5 adult*. One-hour ghost tours of the city. These are group tours only, but if there's availability they will let you join in. Check first.

Guided tours of Cardiff, by local historian John May, **T** 02920 811603, *£5, concession £3. 1½ hours, start from the castle, book in advance*. This walking tour takes in all the main sights in the centre of the city.

Tourist information

Cardiff

Cardiff Visitor Centre, The Old Library, The Hayes, **T** 02920 227281, enquiries@cardifftic.co.uk, visitor@thecardiffinitiative.co.uk, www.visitcardiff.info, *opens 1000-1800 Mon-Sat and 1000-1600 Sun, all year*. Helpful centre with information on both Cardiff and the rest of Wales, with plenty of leaflets/books on activities and places to go. They can also book accommodation for you.

Cardiff Bay Visitor Centre, **T** 02920 463833, *Mon-Fri 0930-1700, Sat, Sun 1030-1700*. Housed in a sort of squashed tin tube down in Cardiff Bay, this has a scale model of the Bay, plenty of information leaflets and also sells parking vouchers.

Passes

If you're exploring outside the city centre, it's worth buying a **CADW Explorer Pass**, *3 days: £9.50 adult, £16.50 for 2 adults, £23 family; 7 days: £15.50 adult, £26 for 2 adults, £32 family*, giving admission to castles like Caerphilly.

South Wales

Penarth TIC, Penarth pier, **T** 02920 708849, *Easter-Sep*. Several different town trail leaflets are available.

Swansea TIC, off West Way by bus station, **T** 01792 468321, www.visitswanseabay.com, tourism@ swansea. gov.uk, *Mon-Sat 0930-1730, Jul/Aug Sun 1000-1600*.

Mumbles TIC, 2 Dunns Lane, T 01792 361302, www.mumbles.info. *Mar-Oct, Mon-Sat 1000-1600 and longer hours in school holidays and Jul and Aug*. Very helpful office with books on walking in the Gower.

Newport TIC, Museum and Art Gallery, John Frost Sq, **T** 01633 842962, newport.tic@newport.gov.uk, *Mon-Sat 0930-1700*.

Vale of Glamorgan Information at council office, 79 Eastgate, Cowbridge, **T** 01446 772901, *Mon, Thu, Fri 0845-1300, 1400-1630 (closes at 1600 Fri)*.

Chepstow TIC, Castle Car Park, Bridge St, **T** 01291 623772, chepstow.tic@monmouthshire.gov.uk, *daily 1000-1730, closed for an hour at lunch*.

Monmouth Visitor Centre, Shire Hall, Agincourt Sq, NP5 3DY, **T** 01600 713899, **F** 01600 772794, www.monmouth.gov.uk, *Easter-Oct 1000-1730, Oct-Easter 1000-1300, 1400-1700*.

Blaenavon TIC ,in the Ironworks, North St, **T** 01495 792615, *Apr-Oct Mon-Fri 0930-1630, Sat 1000-1700, Sun 1000-1630. Follow the signs from the A465*. As well as tourist information they also help people to trace their local family history.

Caerphilly Visitor Centre, Lower Twyn Square, Caerphilly, **T** 02920 880011, tic@caerphilly.gov.uk, *summer Apr-Sep 1000-1800, winter Oct-Mar 1000-1700.*

Merthyr Tydfil TIC, 14a Glebeland St, **T** 01685 379884, merthyrtic@hotmail.com, tic@merthyr.gov.uk, *Apr-Sep 0930-1730 Mon-Sat, Oct-Mar 0900-1700 Mon-Sat.*

Brecon Beacons National Park Information Centre and **Brecon TIC**, Cattle Market Car Park, Brecon, **T** 01874 623156, www.breconbeacons.org. Off the A470 from Cardiff.

Abergavenny TIC, Swan Meadow, Cross St, Abergavenny, **T** 01873 857588, abergavenny.tic@monmouthshire.gov.uk, www.abergavenny.co.uk, *daily Apr-Oct 1000-1730, Nov-Mar 1000-1600, closed for an hour at lunch.*

Hay on Wye TIC, Craft Centre, Oxford Rd, Hay-on-Wye, **T** 01497 820144, post@hay-on-wye.info, www.hay-on-wye.co.uk, *daily Easter-Nov 1000-1300, 1400-1700, rest of year 1100-1300, 1400-1600.*

City Centre 33 The city's ancient heart, a compact and bustling centre that's the commercial and social hub of Cardiff.

Cathays Park 42 The administrative centre, filled with portentous neoclassical buildings and home to a great museum.

Cardiff Bay 48 The old coal port has been transformed from sailortown to sleek marina, and is vying with the centre for the attentions of Cardiff's sassy set.

City suburbs 55 The pretty suburb of Llandaff retains a villagey atmosphere and is home to the city's cathedral, while St Fagans is famous for its open-air museum, complete with stone-domed pigsty, communal oven and cottage built of mud.

City Centre

With its bustling streets, busy shops, and numerous bars and cafés, the centre of Cardiff feels very new – yet this is the oldest part of the city. Roman soldiers once trod this ground, possibly even building their temples on the same sites as are now occupied by the city's shopping malls, today's temples to consumerism. The castle was the site of the Romans' fort, though all that is left to speak of their presence is a section of Roman wall. Later invaders built on the same site, and the castle today, the focus of tourist activity, bears the fingerprints of many generations. Close to the Taff is a more recent addition to the city skyline, the mighty Millennium Stadium, focal point of the city when an important match is being played. Cardiff grinds to a standstill then, and pubs and bars fill with fans sporting Welsh red dragons and enthusiastically sampling pints of Brains – the local brew. Shopping in the centre is a treat, for as well as the modern malls there are numerous atmospheric arcades filled with quirky shops. You can always escape the hordes by strolling along the Taff Walkway that runs behind the Millennium Stadium, or opting for quiet contemplation in a church.

▶▶ *See Sleeping p99, Eating and drinking p120*

◉ Sights

★ Cardiff castle

Castle St, **T** 02920 878100, www.cardiffcastle.com *Daily Mar-Oct 0930-1800, Nov-Feb 0930-1700 – last entry and tour 1 hour before closing. Grounds only £3 adults, £1.90 children, £8.80 family; grounds and tour £6 adults, £3.70 children, £17.60 family. Map 2, D6, p238*

Situated on low ground in the heart of the city, the castle is the historic heart of Cardiff, though it seems slightly incongruous so close to the road and the busy shops and bars. Once inside the

I think my instinct will always be through
the Welsh language...There will be
English influences...but I think the
language of my dreams will
always be Welsh.

Ioan Gruffudd, Cardiff-born actor, Mail on Sunday

high stone walls you can see the motte, or artificial hill, on which is perched the ancient Norman **keep**, the oldest part of the castle buildings dating back to the 11th-century (although the site here was in use even earlier by the Romans). In the Middle Ages, successive owners reinforced and added to this ancient fortification, but many of their additions were demolished in the late 18th century by Capability Brown who had a penchant for 'improving' old buildings.

In the 1420s separate lodgings were built, which became the main living quarters. As the need for defences decreased the house was extended and gradually became more luxurious and comfortable – although it fell into disrepair after the Civil War. Eventually the castle came into the possession of the Bute family, the wealthy Scots who owned vast areas of land in south Wales. By the time the elaborately-monikered John Patrick Crichton-Stuart, 3rd Marquess of Bute (1847-1900) inherited, the family had more money than they knew what to do with – so the Marquess (possibly the richest man in the world at that time) was able to indulge his architectural whims by completely redesigning the house. He commissioned architect William Burges, who shared his passion for the gothic, and the two worked together to create a medieval fantasy that makes Laurence Llewelyn-Bowen look positively restrained. A taster of this style is provided in the façade of the Clock Tower, which is decorated with allegorical statues of the planets and heraldic shields. To see the lavish interior you have to take one of the guided tours, but it's worth it. Decorations are exotic, eccentric and ethereal with monkeys, parrots, knights and nymphs all jostling for your attention. Every riotously colourful room has its

! Part of the castle wall, opposite the Angel Hotel, is decorated with carvings of exotic animals. It once stood by the entrance and was the Marquess of Bute's two-fingered response to the authorities' refusal to allow him to have a menagerie.

The height of bad taste?

Austere, impenetrable fortress overlooking Cardiff from without; exotic, hedonistic palace of riotous colours from within.

own theme. They include the Winter Smoking Room (there was also a Summer Smoking Room) in the Clock Tower, which has stained glass windows, a flamboyant carved chimney piece and richly gilded ceiling. Then there was the Bachelor Bedroom with a luxurious marble bath; the Eastern-influenced Arab Room with intricate patterned ceiling; the Fairytale Nursery, which is decorated with hand-painted tiles depicting stories from the Arabian Nights and the Brothers Grimm; Lord Bute's gilded bedroom with a mirrored ceiling; and the Banqueting Hall where Royals, from Edward VII to Charles and Diana, were entertained. Quiet good taste it ain't but it's certainly worth seeing.

● *If you climb the well-worn steps of the keep you'll get a great panoramic view of the city and surrounding countryside.*

A deserted pigeon house on the top of a truncated sugar loaf.

Unimpressed 18th-century visitor on Capability Brown's 'improvements' to Cardiff's castle keep.

▶ Victorian fantasist

William Burges (1827-1881) was the so-called 'eccentric genius' who realised the Marquess of Bute's extravagant dreams for Cardiff Castle. Burges studied medieval architecture in Europe and travelled widely, soaking up influences from Byzantine, Renaissance and Islamic art.

He adored and idealised the medieval world, which seemed more beautiful, stylish and natural than the vigorously industrial Victorian society he inhabited. He designed grand buildings like Brisbane Cathedral and Cork Cathedral, as well as everyday items such as teapots and chamberpots. He loved using the finest and most luxurious materials, such as marble, amber and cedarwood. When he met the Marquess of Bute he found someone who not only shared his passion for the medieval, but was able to spend lavish amounts of money on bringing a fairytale to life. After the castle, Bute commissioned him to work on Castel Coch, his country retreat. Burges died before it was finished.

St John's Church

St John St, www.stjohncf.btinternet.co.uk *Mon-Sat 1000-1600 and during services on Sun. Free. Map 2, F7, p238*

In amongst the pubs and bars of central Cardiff is this ecclesiastical island: the oldest building in the city centre and the only significant medieval building. The first record of the church was in 1180, though it was rebuilt after Owain Glyndwr's men sacked Cardiff in the mid 15th century. The 130-ft tower dates to about 1475 and is one of the finest examples in Wales of the late perpendicular style. Inside you can see the Herbert Chapel which contains a Jacobean monument to the Herbert brothers, one of whom was Keeper of Cardiff Castle, and the other Private Secretary to Elizabeth I and James I. There's also a Chapel of the Order of St John containing memorials to the great and the good, including Edward VIII (the king who abdicated before he was crowned) and Lord Kitchener, the WWI Commander in Chief famously depicted in contemporary 'Your Country needs YOU' posters. The Victorian stained glass is also considered to be some of the finest in Wales.

● *On pedestrianised Queen St in the city centre is a statue of Aneurin Bevan, the firebrand Labour MP from the Welsh Valleys, who founded the National Health Service.*

The Arcades

Cardiff is one of the best cities in Britain for anyone needing a bit of retail therapy, and these elegant Victorian and Edwardian glass-canopied arcades are one of the jewels of the city. Crammed with individual shops that stock everything from designer clothes and contemporary homewares to Welsh gold rings and Harlech cheese, they were Cardiff's answer to places like the Burlington Arcade in London. They were erected between the 1850s and 1890s and covered existing alleyways. They escaped demolition (the fate of similar structures in other cities) only because Cardiff had little money after the collapse of the coal trade and could not afford redevelopment. The oldest is the Royal Arcade, c1856.

! A peculiar ancient Welsh sport was cnapan. It was played on open ground, had no real rules, and involved hundreds of men battling to take the cnapan, a heavy piece of wood, into the land belonging to one village or another. It was a rough, energetic, good humoured, contact sport. It was also played in the nude.

More than just a sporting venue
The Millennium Stadium, more than any other building or monument, symbolizes Cardiff's – and Wales's – renaissance.

The Millennium Stadium

*Westgate St, **T** 02920 822228,
www.millenniumstadium.co.uk   Shop open Mon-Sat 0930-1700,
tours 1000-1700 run hourly on the hour, booking advised and subject
to events, go to Gate 3 on Westgate St. £5 adults, £2.50 children, £3
conc, £15 family. Near bus station.   Map 2, G-F4, p238*

The top sporting venue in Wales, with seating for 72,500
spectators and a retractable roof that contains a whopping 8,000
tons of steel. It was built on the site of the old National Stadium
that stood on the famous Cardiff Arms Park. It's now the home of
Welsh rugby and hosts matches in the annual Six Nations
Championship, as well as international football matches. In the
embarrassing absence (for the English) of a football stadium at
Wembley, it is also the place for major English footballing events
including the FA Cup Final. Take a tour to see the dressing rooms,
the tunnel, the Royal box and, of course, the pitch.

Cathays Park

*The area occupied by Cathays Park was sold to Cardiff by the
wealthy Bute family in 1898. It was turned into the centre of
administrative power, with serious and impressive buildings
arranged around the National War Memorial and broad, tree-lined
boulevards cutting through the smooth grass. The grandest building
is the **City Hall**, which was officially opened in 1905 by Edward VII,
who at the same time gave Cardiff official city status. It's an area
that has a rather sedate feel, a serene and green corner of the city
centre. The area's main feature is the **National Museum and Gallery**,
one of Cardiff's greatest assets. The university is also here – and the
surrounding student districts of **Cathays** and **Roath** have lots of
reasonably priced places to eat.*

▸▸ *See Sleeping City suburbs, p103, Eating and drinking p124.*

◉ Sights

★ National Museum and Gallery

Cathays Park, **T** 02920 397951, www.nmgw.ac.uk *Tue-Sun 1000-1700. Free. Cathays is the nearest train station.*
Map 2, C8/9, p238

This excellent museum and art gallery could hold its head up anywhere in the world. It covers everything from a hi-tech, interactive look at the Evolution of Wales – a good spot for children on a rainy day – to conventional displays of art.

The story of Wales is told through its archaeology and natural history. There are galleries on animals and the environment, Viking-Age crosses, finds from Crannogs, displays on the early church and some beautiful Celtic jewellery. There are also some Roman relics found in Wales, which include delicate statuettes of dogs. The section on Wales in the Middle Ages includes the Levelinus Stone which was raised between 1198 and 1230 by the monks of Aberconwy Abbey in Gwynedd to commemorate a gift of land from Llywelyn the Great. It's inscribed with a mixture of Welsh and Latin.

If you're a connoisseur of china then head upstairs to the extensive collection of Welsh ceramics – it contains around 3,000 pieces of Welsh pottery and porcelain. But if you're short of time give it a miss and focus on the **art collection** instead. It is intended to illustrate the art history of Wales and put it in context – and as you would expect, contains many works by Welsh artists from Thomas Jones and Richard Wilson 1713-82 (the first painter to capture the Welsh landscape on canvas) to Augustus John and Ceri Richards. Gallery 5 focuses on Art in Wales from 1780-1860.

There are also works by Poussin, Cuyp, Claude and Canaletto. British artists in general are well represented and there's a good

Good Impression

The National Museum and Gallery boasts a collection of French Impressionist paintings to rival any gallery in the UK.

selection of works by Pre-Raphaelites such as Dante Gabriel Rossetti, Ford Madox Brown and Burne-Jones.

In Gallery 3 look out for the large **tapestry cartoons**. These have aroused some controversy in the art world as they were once thought to be the sole work of Rubens, but now no-one is sure to what extent the master worked on them. They were produced by his workshop – but this was a major commercial operation, something like a modern design studio. Rubens certainly died before they were finished.

The jewel in the gallery is the **Davies collection** of 19th- and early 20th-century French art, the bequest of Gwendoline and Margaret Davies. It's a remarkable collection by two sisters, and one of the best collections of Impressionist art in the UK. Room 12 contains several sculptures by Rodin, including a large copy of *The Kiss*; a Degas bronze of a dancer, and paintings by Boudin, Manet, Monet and Pissarro. There's also Renoir's *La Parisienne* (1874) better known as 'The Blue Lady'. Room 13 has Van Gogh's *Rain – Auvers* 1890, as well as paintings by Cézanne. Look out for the small picture of *A Shepherdess* by Anton Mauve – he gave painting lessons to Van Gogh. Galleries 14 and 15 focus on 20th-century art, with Magritte, Lucien Freud, Stanley Spencer and others all represented. There's also a gallery that has a changing collection of contemporary art, which features Welsh artists as well as people like Rachel Whiteread.

In Gallery 15 there's a view of Six Bells Colliery, Abertillery in Ebbw Fach Valley, painted by **LS Lowry**. He was taken to Wales by his Welsh friend and patron Monty Bloom.

! It's often said that one hundred years ago, Cardiff was the
• energy equivalent of the Persian Gulf. The international price of coal was set in the Cardiff Coal Exchange, in what is now Cardiff Bay.

City Hall

Cathays Park, **T** 02920 872000/871727, www.cardiff.gov.uk *Open Mon-Fri office hours, sometimes on Sat – no access if a function is taking place. Free. Cathays is the nearest station.* Map 2, C8, p238

This is Cardiff's answer to the White House, the heart of the Civic Centre built at the start of the 20th century when Cardiff was a wealthy coal port. It's a confident neo-classical building, the focus of civic pride, with a façade of white Portland stone and an ornate clock tower. On the large dome is a snarling Welsh dragon that looks as if it's guarding a precious egg – presumably Wales. The bells in the clock tower are engraved, some in Welsh and some in English. The interior is impressive and well worth a look. Various paintings hang from the walls including a triple portrait of Princess Diana, painted when she still had her Royal HRH title. The Marble Hall is lined with columns of Siena marble and statues depicting 'Heroes of Wales'. Each statue is by a different sculptor, and the figures represented include Owain Glyndwr, Harri Tewdwr (Henry VII), St David and Boudicca (Boadicea) – the woman who led the Celtic Iceni tribe in revolt against the Romans. Nearby buildings that help to make up the Civic Centre include the Welsh National War Memorial and the Temple of Peace.

In the main entrance to City Hall is a statue of a woman carrying a young child and wearing a chain round her waist. It commemorates the 36 women, four children and six men who in 1981 marched from Cardiff to Berkshire to protest against the siting of American cruise missiles at RAF Greenham Common. The site became known worldwide as a focus of anti-nuclear protest.

The desire for autonomy

It was in the mid 19th century that the modern campaign for greater autonomy for Wales really began. There was a revival of interest in Welsh culture – as evidenced by the reintroduction of the eisteddfod into Welsh life – the first being the National Eisteddfod of 1858. In 1885 the Welsh Language Society was started, which succeeded in ensuring that Welsh (which had been banned) was taught in schools, and a political movement for a separate Wales was formed in 1886 as part of the Liberal party. The political scene in Wales became increasingly radical and in 1900 Merthyr Tydfil elected a Scot, **Keir Hardie** as their MP – Britain's first Labour MP. WW1 saw a Welshman, **David Lloyd George** become Prime Minister. The Labour Party continued to grow in importance in Wales, but there was dissatisfaction at their failure to introduce Home Rule

– and the lack of safeguards for the Welsh language. In 1925 **Plaid Cymru**, the National Party of Wales, was established. One of the founders was Saunder Lewis. He and two other Plaid members – DJ Williams and Lewis Valentine – gained notoriety (and Welsh support) when they set fire to buildings at an RAF station in North Wales. Over the years demands for home rule increased again and in 1979 a **referendum** was held – the result was a huge disappointment for the nationalists, with 80% of people voting against a Welsh assembly. After the Thatcher government was finally defeated and Labour took power again, another referendum was held in 1997. This time there was a tiny majority in favour, and elections to the **National Assembly for Wales** took place in May 1999. Unlike the Scottish Parliament, it has no tax-raising powers.

★ Cardiff Bay

About a mile from the city centre, Cardiff Bay is the city's former docklands area, built in the 19th century by the Bute family, and the key to the city's growth and wealth. It's separated from the city by parallel streets: Bute Street – to the west of which are the poor, multi-racial areas of Butetown and Grangetown; and Lloyd George Avenue – a characterless stretch lined with bland, and pricey, new housing. Once better known as Tiger Bay, this was a cosmopolitan, working-class area, home to people from all over Britain as well as around 50 other nations including Somalis, Scandinavians, Russians and Indians. After the decline of the docks, the area became increasingly run down, but has now been given a serious – and expensive – facelift. It's now full of hope and energy with shiny new buildings going up all the time, retail outlets, and a liberal splash of bars and restaurants. It has certainly helped regenerate the area, although the downside is the consequent loss of its working-class character and sense of community. It feels very different to the rest of Cardiff, a shiny new appendage that hasn't yet grown on to the main body. But it's the site of the new Welsh Assembly building, as well as the Welsh Millennium Centre – which will be home to the National Opera – and there are loads of bars and restaurants, many of which offer outdoor seating with views of the water, a very pleasant option on a fine sunny day.

Further developments in the Bay will include a £700 million International Sports Village. The first phase of this will involve construction of an Olympic-standard swimming pool, with plans for a snowdome and an ice arena. There's enough to see and do to occupy you for the best part of a day and it's changing all the time. The centre of the waterfront is taken up with the shops, bars and restaurants of the new Mermaid Quay development. From here you can get boat trips into the Bay and out to the Barrage.

▸▸ *See Sleeping p102, Eating and drinking p125*

Down there was Tiger Bay, the district between the docks and the tidal flats known vividly as East Mud: one of the best-known and toughest of all the world's sailor towns…

Jan Morris, Wales, (Penguin, 2000)

● Sights

National Assembly Exhibition

Cardiff Bay, **T** 02920 898200, www.wales.gov.uk *Mon-Thu 0930-1630, Fri 1000-1630, Sat, Sun 1000-1700. Free. Bus 6 Bay Xpress. Map 3, G3, p240*

This exhibition is housed in the lovely redbrick Victorian Pierhead Building on the waterfront, which is topped with a distinctive clock tower and contains fine stonework and tiling. It was built in 1897 as home for the Bute Dock Company. This exhibition focuses on the background to the setting up of the Assembly, an explanation of devolution and how the Assembly operates. There's also a scale model of the new Assembly building, which is currently being erected on adjacent land: work, it is hoped, will finish late in 2005. For now the Assembly functions from a nearby building and tours to see it in action can be arranged (**T** 02920 898477).

Techniquest

Stuart St, **T** 02920 475475, www.techniquest.org *Mon-Fri 0930-1630, Sat, Sun 1030-1700, school holidays Mon-Fri 0930-1700. £6.75 adults, £4.65 children, £18.50 family. Bus 6 Bay Xpress. Map 3, G1, p240*

This is a family-friendly, interactive science centre with a whole load of 'hands-on' exhibits covering everything from firing a rocket to forecasting the weather. In the 'wet' area exhibits range from building a dam to the importance of recycling water. There's a planetarium, where a changing programme of audio-visual presentations covers matters such as light pollution, and whether or not the moon landings were faked by the Americans. At weekends and during holidays, demonstrations are held in the Science Theatre, covering themes like dinosaurs and inventions.

Pioneering spirit
Cardiff's rich merchants supported Captain Scott's polar expedition; his spirit of adventure is celebrated in the Bay today.

Scott Memorial
Millennium Waterfront. *Bus 6, Bay Xpress.* Map 3, H3, p240

In 1910 Captain Scott's ill-fated expedition to the South Pole set sail from Cardiff on the *Terra Nova*. The trip was largely funded by Cardiff's mercantile community (wealthy patrons in the other parts of Britain having got rather tired of stumping up with the readies for his polar explorations), and a grand farewell banquet was held in the city before they left. Scott didn't sail with them on the first leg of the no doubt extremely uncomfortable journey – he travelled by luxury steamer and joined them later. There's a memorial to the explorers near the Norwegian church in the Bay and also in Roath Park.

! They say that 200 rugby pitches would fit into the area
• occupied by the Bay.

Shock of the Bay
Though not to everyone's taste, the Barrage has effectively sculpted Cardiff's post-industrial landscape.

Norwegian Church
Millennium Waterfront, **T** 02920 454899. *Daily 1000-1600. Free. Bus 6, Bay Xpress. Map 3, H3, p240*

An incongruous sight amongst the Victorian red brick and contemporary glittering glass, this church is a reminder that Cardiff was once an internationally important seaport. With its white wooden walls and black roof, it looks rather quaint and rustic. It was originally a Norwegian Church and Seamen's Mission and was moved here from a former site in the Bay. It's now an arts centre and café (see entertainment).
 ● *The author Roald Dahl was baptised here. He was born in Cardiff, but his father was Norwegian.*

► Old King Coal

Cardiff might have remained a small coastal town had it not been for the Industrial Revolution, which dramatically transformed it from backwater to big city. The metamorphosis was largely due to the local landowners, the Scottish Bute family, who owned much of the land in both Cardiff and the surrounding coal-rich valleys. The first Marquess built the Glamorganshire Canal in 1794 linking Cardiff with Merthyr Tydfil in the valleys. This was a far quicker and cheaper way of transporting coal than the previous method – mules. The second Marquess built the first dock on the Taff, soon followed by several more, and a lucrative export trade in 'black diamonds' was established.

King Coal made Cardiff one of the busiest ports in the world – and the Butes, who were in a position to insist that only their docks be used for trading Valleys' coal, one of the richest families. As the Welsh travel writer Jan Morris put it: '…from…his castle at the top of the town, the Marquis looked over the rooftops of his indefatigable fief – to the sea one way, where the coal of Wales went streaming off to the markets of the world, to the hills the other, where in valleys hidden from his view the miners toiled to dig it out.'

Butetown History and Arts Centre

4/5 Dock Chambers, Bute St, **T** 02920 256757, www.bhac.org *Tue-Fri 1000-1700, Sat, Sun 1100-1630. Free. Cardiff Bay station or bus 6, Bay Xpress. Map 3, E3, p240*

A small, but fascinating, gallery which focuses on the multi-racial history of the Bay. There are changing exhibitions of photographs and documents, with a lot of emphasis on local memories and stories.

Close to Butetown Arts Centre there's a huge steel fountain, on the other side of which is the new face of Cardiff Bay – the **Wales Millennium Centre**, due to open Nov 2004. This will be an international arts centre, home to Welsh National Opera and a venue for everything from ballet to musicals.

Goleulong 2000 Lightship

Harbour Drive, **T** 02920 487609, www.welcome.to/lightship2000 *Mon-Sat 1000-1700, Sun 1400-1700. Free. Bus 6, Bay Xpress.*
Map 3, H4, p240

This lightship (*goleulong* in Welsh) was in use until the early 1990s, warning shipping off dangerous areas on Britain's treacherous coast. It used to be manned with a crew of seven who would be airlifted in and out by helicopter. You can see their cabins, and the light. The ship now contains a chapel and a Christian café.

Cardiff Bay Barrage

Cardiff Bay, **T** 02920 700234, www.cardiffharbour.com. *Daily 0800-2000 Apr-Sep, reduced hours in winter. Free. From land train or waterbus from Cardiff Bay.*
Off Map 3, boats leave from Map 3, G2, p240

This striking – and controversial – structure was built across the Taff and Ely estuaries to keep the tide out and create the enormous lake which forms the heart of the Bay development. The barrage, which cost over £200 million to build, is an advanced piece of engineering with locks, sluice gates and a fish

! Property in the Bay is expensive, but doesn't guarantee
• privacy. Charlotte Church bought one of the showpiece flats here, only to discover that she was on the tourist bus route – easily glimpsed by those sitting on the top deck.

Best **Things for free**

- The Impressionist paintings at the National Museum and Gallery, p43
- The Museum of Welsh Life, p57
- Poetry at the Dylan Thomas Centre in Swansea, p67
- Relaxing on the Gower's beaches, p71
- Window-shopping in the Arcades, p172

pass. It allowed the marina to be developed but meant that a huge expanse of mudflats – a precious habitat for thousands of wading birds – disappeared. The birds you're most likely to spot today are the resident swans and cormorants. On a clear day the views from the barrage are superb – you can see right across the Bristol Channel to England – and if you come late September-December, you might well see salmon leaping up the fish pass as they return to spawn in the waters of the Taff. You can get here by boat from Mermaid Quay or walk here from Penarth.

Cardiff suburbs

Only part of Cardiff since 1922, Llandaff – the 'place on the Taff' – retains a distinctive, villagey feel. Its attraction for visitors is that it's the site of Llandaff cathedral, the city's most famous church, which is tucked away in a sheltered hollow surrounded by grass and trees. The village of St Fagans, four miles west of the city centre, is quite picturesque, but what visitors come to see is the Museum of Welsh Life. It's situated in the grounds of St Fagans Castle, a Grade 1 listed building that dates back to Elizabethan times. In 1946 the Earl of Plymouth donated the castle and its surrounding land to the National Museum of Wales – on condition that they build an open-air museum there.

▸▸ *See Sleeping p102, Eating and drinking p125*

▶ Kiss and tell

If you hear anyone mention SWS, (pronounced swoos), it stands for Social, Welsh and Sexy (www.swsuk.com) – a sort of social club for ex-pat Welsh people, and anyone else who's got an interest in Wales (you don't have to be sexy either). They've got branches in London, New York and Moscow and members include Catherine Zeta-Jones and Ioan Gruffudd. Sws is also Welsh for kiss. They've set up their own dating agency too – www.cwtsh.com, but don't think you'll get a date with Ioan...

◉ Sights

Llandaff Cathedral

Llandaff, **T** 02920 564554, www.llandaffcathedral.org.uk *Daily. Free. Approximately 2 miles north west of city centre along Cathedral Rd. Buses from city centre.* Map 1, B6, p240

The cathedral at Llandaff is Cardiff's most important religious site. It stands on the site of a sixth-century church, founded by St Teilo, although the present building dates from the 12th century when the Norman stone church was built by Bishop Urban. The cathedral suffered following the Reformation and by the 18th century was almost a ruin. However it was saved by restoration work, particularly in the mid 19th century, when Pre-Raphaelite artists made a great contribution to its renewal. There's a triptych *The Seed of David* by Dante Gabriel Rossetti (with figures modelled by his friends William Morris – King

❗ Famously bad-tempered international diva, Shirley Bassey was born in Tiger Bay.

David; Jane Burden, his wife – the Virgin Mary; and Burne-Jones – a shepherd), and stained glass by William Morris and Burne-Jones. The cathedral was badly damaged in 1941 and further restoration and rebuilding was undertaken. An enormous Jacob Epstein statue, *Christ in Majesty*, was added during this period.

Museum of Welsh Life

St Fagans, **T** 02920 573500. *Daily 1000-1700. Free. Bus 32 or 320, about every hour from city centre, less frequent on Sundays. Taxis cost around £10. Map 1, C, p236*

This excellent open-air museum is four miles west of the city centre in the grounds of St Fagans Castle, and could easily take up a full day – especially if you've got kids. The museum brings to life 500 years of Welsh social history. The **indoor galleries** (handy if it's raining) include a wide collection of agricultural implements; a costume gallery with traditional Welsh clothing; a fascinating section on folklore – including elder tree crosses, believed to give protection against witches; and displays of gruesome looking old surgical instruments. **Outdoors**, around 44 acres (18 ha) of ground have been given over to a collection of 40 period Welsh buildings, moved from their original locations and carefully rebuilt here. They come together to give an evocative glimpse of old Wales. The buildings range from tiny **Nant Wallter Cottage**, a two room, 18th century thatched cottage with walls made of clay/mud mixed with straw and stone dust, to **Kennixton Farmhouse**, a comfortable 17th century farmhouse with red painted walls – for protection against evil spirits. There's also a chapel, a cockpit, a stylish stone pigsty, a

! Founding father – in 1713, Francis Lewis, one of the signatories to the American Declaration of Independence, was born in Llandaff

mill, a Victorian school and a recreated Celtic village. Perhaps most fascinating are the **Rhyd-Y-Car** ironworker's houses, a 19th century terrace from Merthyr Tydfil complete with gardens and sheds. Each of the six houses is furnished in a different period, ranging from 1805 to 1985. Close by there's a post-war **pre-fab bungalow**, an example of the kit homes that were constructed to replace houses bombed in the Second World War.

St Fagans castle itself is furnished as it would have been at the end of the 19th century. It is in the process of being refurbished, following problems with the roof, but should be fully open by summer 2004. It's got some fine tapestries, dark wood panelling and a red silk bed. When you've exhausted all the buildings you can also explore the lovely **Castle Gardens**, with terraces, 18th century fishponds and a recently restored **Italian Garden**.

⬤ *The Victorian **Gwalia Stores** are a great place to browse. You'll find things like bile beans, Sloan's liniment, loose biscuits and tins labelled: Ringer's Shag – The Old Favourite.*

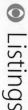

Museums and galleries in Cardiff

- **National Museum and Gallery** Houses the finest collection of Impressionist works outside France, p43.
- **National Assembly Exhibition** Not-as-dull-as-it-sounds exhibition on the new Welsh Assembly, p50.
- **Techniquest** Hands-on, have fun as you learn, science centre, p50.
- **Butetown History and Arts Centre** Small space with pictures and memories of multi-racial life in the old docks, p53.
- **Museum of Welsh Life** Open air museum with buildings from all over Wales, p57.
- **Craft in the Bay** A retail gallery showcasing contemporary arts in Wales, p173.

Museums and galleries in South Wales

- **Turner House Gallery**, Penarth. Displays the work of Ffotogallery, the national agency for contemporary and historic Welsh photographs, p64.
- **Cosmeston Medieval Village**, Lavernock Point. Reconstructed 14th-century village, where tour guides will show you round wearing medieval dress, p65.
- **Dylan Thomas Centre**, Swansea. Celebration of Dylan Thomas with manuscripts, letters, memorabilia, literary festivals and events, p67.
- **Swansea Museum**, Swansea. Might be the oldest museum in Wales, complete with mummy! Also has a good collectionof Nantgarw pottery and porcelain, p67.

Museums and galleries in South Wales

Listings

- **Egypt Centre**, Swansea. Part of the university, this extensive collection of Egyptian artefacts includes jewellery, statues and over a thousand items in total, p68.
- **Glynn Vivian Art Gallery**, Swansea. Collection of Welsh art, porcelain and ceramics, p68.
- **Carmarthenshire County Museum**, Abergwilli. Showcases regional history, including castles, pottery and archaeological finds, p74.
- **Chepstow Museum**, Chepstow. Local history, p82.
- **Usk Rural Life Museum**, Usk. Fascinating museum of rural life, housed in three converted barns and tracing the path of rural life from 1850 to the end of the Second World War, p85.
- **Nelson Museum and Local History Centre**, Monmouth. Nelson memorabilia, including a false glass eye, p85.
- **Big Pit National Mining Museum**, Blaenavon. Insight into the life of Welsh miners. The highlight of a visit is the tour underground to see the conditions in which miners used to work, p89.
- **Margam Stones Museum**, near Port Talbot. Collection of early Christian stone sculptures, p91.
- **Oriel Jazz Gallery**, Brecon. Examines the development of jazz, and the centre of the town's annual Jazz Festival. Nice... p94
- **South Wales Borderers Museum**, Brecon. Home to the regiment that fought at Rorkes' Drift in 1879, p94.

Vale of Glamorgan

*Tucked away in the corner south west of Cardiff is the gentle, pastoral scenery of the Vale of Glamorgan. It's easily accessible from the city, with trains to Bridgend, buses to towns like Cowbridge and a water bus to Penarth. In 2005 the Vale of Glamorgan train line should open between Cardiff and Bridgend, stopping at places like Llantwit Major. The heritage coastline is varied, with the fish, chips and fairground rides resort of Barry mingling with the pleasant, but decidedly snoozy, Victorian town of Penarth. There are craggy cliffs, some award-winning beaches and good walks – notably the coastal walk around Dunraven Bay. Inland is **Cowbridge**, a pretty and very prosperous town (think Surrey with a Welsh accent) filled with independent shops, including lots of antique shops, and some good places to eat. A great little place to stroll around and window shop, though don't expect to find any bargains.*

▸▸ *See Sleeping p105, Eating and drinking p128*

 Sights

Llantwit Major

A little village (**TIC**, Town Hall, **T** 01446 796086) where you'll find **St Illtud's Church**, off Burial Lane. St Illtud founded a church and religious school on this site around 500 AD. It was the first Christian college in Britain – and alumni are said to include St David and St Patrick. Local kings were buried here and the church contains an important collection of Celtic stones. The building you see today dates back to Norman times.

A couple of miles from the town is **St Donat's Castle**, a medieval pile which was bought by American newspaper tycoon William Randolph Hearst in 1925. Various well known names stayed there including Charlie Chaplin, Bing Crosby, Marilyn Monroe and JFK. It's now home to **Atlantic College**, the international school (tours available in Aug, ring **T** 01446 799010 to book, charge), and also the **St Donat's Art Centre** (**T** 01446 799100, www.stdonats.com), which hosts various festivals (see festivals) as well as acting as a venue for theatre, film and dance events.

Llantwit Major is close to **Nash Point**, a lovely lonely spot with two lighthouses, craggy cliffs and a warning bell floating in the bay, clanging eerily in the wind. Travel west along the coast and you come to **Ogmore by Sea**, where there's a lovely sandy beach that's a real favourite with **kite surfers**.

Penarth

Penarth is a Victorian seaside town with a small promenade, a rather genteel little pier and a good vegetarian restaurant (see eating). It's linked to Cardiff by water bus and in summer you can also take trips on the **Waverley**, the world's last sea-going paddle steamer (ask the helpful **TIC** on the pier for details, **T** 02920 708849, Easter-Sep, several different town trail leaflets are available). The town also contains the **Turner House Gallery** (1 Plymouth Rd, **T** 02920 708870, www.ffotogallery.org, Wed-Sun 1100-1700, free), which displays the works of Ffotogallery – a national agency for contemporary and historic Welsh photographs. In the cemetery is the grave of Saunders Lewis, the playwright and one of the founders of Plaid Cymru.

Lavernock Point

At the little church at **Lavernock Point**, near Penarth, is a plaque informing you that in 1897 'near this spot the first radio waves were

! French impressionist painter Alfred Sisley came to Penarth in 1897 and stayed for four weeks at 4 Clive Place. The town and its seafront feature in a number of his works.

exchanged across water by Guglielmo Marconi and George Kemp/Between Lavernock and Flat Holm'. The historic message was disappointingly prosaic in content: 'Are you ready?' – not much better than 'Testing, Testing' really. **Flat Holm** is a tiny island, once a retreat for monks, refuge for smugglers – and reputedly the burial place of the murderers of Thomas à Beckett. It has Viking associations and was mentioned in the Anglo Saxon Chronicles as Bradan Relice. It's a Site of Special Scientific Interest and a Nature Reserve, home to Wales' largest colony of gulls.

Cosmeston Medieval Village

Lavernock Rd, **T** 02920 701678. *Nov-Mar 1100-1600 (last tour 1500), Apr-Oct 1100-1700 (last tour 1600). £3 adult, £2 child. South of Penarth on B4267.*

Go back to the days of the plague at this reconstructed 14th-century village. The original village grew up around a fortified manor house, but began to decline during the Black Death and was eventually deserted. It was rediscovered during archaeological work, and gradually recreated on the excavated ruins. Villagers in medieval costume give tours, and it's a good place to bring kids.

Kenfig Nature Reserve

Near Porthcawl, **T** 01656 743386, www.kenfig.org.uk. *Open daily 0900-1700, Visitor Centre 1400-1630. Free. 3 miles north of Porthcawl.*

Bug lovers and botanists will love this National Nature Reserve which covers 1,300 acres of ground. **Kenfig Pool** is an enormous freshwater lake and forms the heart of the reserve. It provides a habitat for migratory birds as well as many rare plants and insects. Among the 13 species of orchid that grow here is the rare Fen Orchid, while the site has a special claim to fame: it even has its own unique species of weevil.

Dyffryn Gardens

St Nicholas, Vale of Glamorgan, **T** 02920 593328,
www.dyffryngardens.org.uk *Easter-Sep 1000-1800, Oct 1000-1700.*
£3.50, £7 family, free in winter. Off the A48.

These are Grade 1 listed Edwardian gardens around a grand
country house. There are lawns, fountains, an herbaceous border,
Italian garden, arboretum and physic garden. In the 1900s
Reginald Cory, a former owner of the estate, helped to sponsor
several plant hunting expeditions which brought rare and exotic
species back to Dyffryn. In the arboretum is a huge Paper Bark
Maple (Acer griseum) which was grown from a seed collected in
China by Ernest Wilson, a famous plant hunter.

Swansea (Abertawe) and around

*Swansea is the second city of Wales, and Welsh is far more widely
spoken here than in its great rival Cardiff. The city's origins go back
to Norman times at least and in the 18th century it became a
thriving coal port. Badly damaged by bombing in WW2 it's not likely
to inspire you to try out that new digital camera, but it's got some
worthwhile museums and will eventually be the location for the
new Welsh Waterfront museum. The traditional Labour Club on
Wind Street now rubs shoulders with sharp bars and restaurants – a
sign of the changes the city's undergoing. If you've only a day to
spend here try not to make it Monday – nearly all the sights close.
West of Swansea Bay, and the gateway to the Gower, is the cheery
stretch of seafront known, unenticingly, as Mumbles. Now famous
as the birthplace of Catherine Zeta-Jones who's building a £3
million house here, it offers a great choice of places to eat and drink.*
▶▶ *See Sleeping p106, Eating and drinking p130*

◉ Sights

Dylan Thomas Centre

Somerset Place, Swansea, **T** 01792 463980,
www.swansea.gov.uk/dylanthomas, www.dylanthomas.org *Open
1030-1630 Tues-Sun. Free. Off the A4067, buses from Cardiff.*

This beautiful colonnaded Victorian listed building celebrates
Thomas through memorabilia like original manuscripts and letters,
and also hosts literature festivals, author readings, lectures and
discussions. It's got a good second-hand bookshop and a nice café.

Swansea Museum

Victoria Rd, **T** 01792 653763, www.swanseagov.uk. *Tue-Sun
1030-1730. Free. Off the A4067.*

Possibly the oldest museum in Wales (Dylan Thomas called it "a
museum that should be in a museum"), it's best known for its
ancient 2,200-year-old mummy of a priest called Hor, but also
has a good collection of Nantgarw pottery and porcelain. There's
also a memorial to Edgar Evans, a Swansea man who was one of
Captain Scott's companions on the ill-fated polar expedition.

Swansea market

Off Castle Square, by the Quadrant Shopping Centre. *Mon-Sat
0930-1700. Off the A4067.*

Swansea's salty maritime heritage means you can come here to try
local grub such as fresh cockles with loads of vinegar and pepper.

! Dylan Thomas was born at 5 Cwmdonkin Drive, in the upstairs
● front bedroom, on 26 October 1914. The house can be visited
by special arrangement with the Dylan Thomas Centre.

The biggest covered market in Wales, it's also renowned for fresh seafood from the estuary, Welsh cheese, laverbread and bacon (Swansea's traditional breakfast dish) and freshly-baked welshcakes. Joe's Ice Cream, also available in nearby Mumbles (where they even queue in the winter), is proclaimed by locals (and many sweet-toothed visitors) to be the best ice cream in the whole world.

● *While in Swansea try the local delicacy – laverbread. It's a type of seaweed, collected from the coast and cooked in oatmeal. It's eaten with bacon or ham and is said to be highly nutritious.*

Egypt Centre

Taliesin Arts Centre, Swansea University, **T** 01792 295960, www.swansea.ac.uk/egypt *Tue-Sat 1000-1600. Free. Singleton Campus, off the A4067 to Mumbles.*

There are over 1,000 Egyptian artefacts dating as far back as 3500 BC, with statues of gods and goddesses, jewellery and the painted coffin of a musician from Thebes. Interesting even if you wouldn't know Tutankhamen from Nefertiti.

Glynn Vivian Art Gallery

Alexandra Rd, **T** 01792 655006. *Tue-Sun 1030-1700. Free. Off A4118.*

The gallery has an excellent collection of work by 20th-century Welsh artists such as Ceri Richards, and Gwen and Augustus John. There's also an internationally important collection of Welsh porcelain and china.

Singleton Botanical Gardens

Off Gower Rd, Sketty, **T** 01792 298637. *Daily, winter 0900-1700, summer 0900-1800, Aug 0900-2000. Free. Bus 18, 20, 21A.*

The gardens have glass houses for desert, temperate and tropical regions, as well as a herb garden, huge magnolias and

Grape Expectations

It might sound unlikely but there are now several vineyards in Wales, clustered together in the south-east corner. Several Welsh wines have even won medals at various international competitions.

It was the Romans who introduced wine making to Wales and one of their largest British vineyards was at Caerleon, where fossilised grape pips have been found. Later the monks at Tintern Abbey produced their own wines, but when Henry VIII dissolved the monasteries the tradition died out.

It was revived by the fabulously wealthy Marquess of Bute who sent his gardener to France to do some research into it, and then planted his first vineyard in 1875 at his country home of Castell Coch.

More vineyards were established and became reasonably successful – in 1887 3,600 bottles were produced for Queen Victoria's golden jubilee.

Production later faltered, particularly during WW1, and it wasn't until the mid 20th century that wine-growing began again. Most Welsh wines are white, but some rosés are also being produced.

Vineyards
Cariad Wines:
Llanerch Vineyard, Hensol, Pendoylan, **T** 01443 225877, www.llanerch-vineyard.co.uk Easter-end Oct, daily 1000-1700, £3, is the largest vineyard in Wales with a six-acre vineyard and 10 acres of landscaped grounds. A tour includes a wine tasting.

Tintern Parva Wines:
Parva Farm, Tintern (**T** 01291 689636, daily 1030-1830) features two acres of vines on a 60-acre working farm. Free tastings are on offer in the shop, while the self-guided vineyard tour is £1.

Keep it clean!

All Saints Church in Oystermouth was built on the site of an old Roman villa. Buried in the graveyard is Thomas Bowdler (1754-1825), the original man with a blue pencil. He became famous as the prudish editor of the *Family Shakespeare* in which he removed '...words and expressions...which cannot with propriety be read aloud in a family' – ie he took out all the rude bits. Hence the following term emerged: 'to bowdlerize'.

ornamental gardens. And in the economic greenhouse you can see lots of exotic plants that are of economic importance, such as sugar cane, olives, rice, coffee and coconut.

Clyne Gardens

Mill Lane, Blackpill, **T** 01792 401737, www.swansea.gov.uk/leisure/allparks.html *Daily, all year. Free. Bus 14,3,2, 2A.*

This is largely a woodland garden and covers 46 acres of land surrounding **Clyne Castle**. As well as a great collection of rhododendrons and azaleas (it's at its best in May), there's a bog garden, wildflower meadow and bluebell wood. It's a good place to bring kids and picnic.

Mumbles (Mwmbwls)

Dylan Thomas called Mumbles 'a rather nice village, despite its name'. The unfortunate name originally referred to a couple of little offshore islands and is a corruption of the name *mamelles* (breasts) that French sailors gave them. Today it's a general term for the village of Oystermouth (Ystumllwynarth), an historic oyster-fishing port, and the long stretch of seafront to Mumbles Lighthouse and the blue flag beach Bracelet Bay. It's noted for its generous number of pubs (some patronized by the ever-thirsty Mr Thomas) and has some great places to eat. Nearby **Caswell Bay** offers some great urban surfing. The winding streets behind the promenade hide the ruins of **Oystermouth Castle**, off Newton Rd, www.castlewales.com Easter-end Sep daily 1000-1800. £1, concessions £0.80, a former Norman stronghold.

★ The Gower (Gwyr)

West of Mumbles is the 19-mile long Gower (Gwyr), a small and scenic peninsula, which resembles a toe dipping tentatively into the Bristol Channel. The Gower was Britain's first designated Area of Outstanding Natural Beauty and much of the coastline is owned by the National Trust. Its lovely beaches have become a favourite with surfers and windsurfers (for surfing try Llangennith, especially if you're a beginner; for windsurfing try Oxwich Bay – again good for learners, Horton and Llangennith). Its cliff tops and narrow lanes offer some good walking – there's a Gower Coastal Path – and great cycling. The peninsula is sprinkled with ancient churches, small villages and lovely heathlands. If you want to escape the crowds make for the north coast, where there are lonely stretches of grazed saltmarshes, rich in rare plants.

▸▸ *See Sleeping p108, Eating and drinking p132*

!
• Mumbles' most famous daughter is Hollywood actress Catherine Zeta-Jones, who still returns occasionally to see her family and has just built a £3 million house in the town – much to the delight of visiting rubber-neckers.

Sights

Three Cliffs Bay

Three Cliffs Bay is the closest of the Gower beaches to Swansea. At nearby Parkmill, on the main A4118, is the **Gower Heritage Centre** (**T** 01792 371206, www.gowerheritagecentre.co.uk, daily, *Apr-Oct 1000-1730, 1000-1600 Nov-Mar, £3.60 adults, £2.50 children, £11 family*), a child-orientated attraction based around an old water-powered corn mill, with craft workshops and displays, and a tea shop. It's low-key stuff and if you think you are going to be pushed for time, you'd be better off heading out to the beach or out to Rhossili instead.

Oxwich Bay

Oxwich Bay is a National Nature Reserve encompassing dunes, marshes and woodlands, as well as a popular sandy beach. Here you'll find **St Illtyd's Church** (*generally open 1100-1500*), which stands on the site of a sixth-century Celtic monastic cell.

● *The Gower's dotted with pretty and historic little churches. If you're interested in things ecclesiastical pick up a copy of the leaflet 'In the Steps of the Saints' which has details of all the Gower's churches. These include St Cadoc's, Cheriton, known as the Cathedral of the Gower, and St Mary's, Pennard burial place of Welsh poet Harri Webb.*

Rhossili

From popular Port Eynon, a Blue Flag beach, you can walk a lovely stretch of coastline round to Rhossili. Rhossili is a stunning area – the Land's End of the Gower (but without the ghastly commercialism that has ruined the one in Cornwall). Much of it is owned by the National Trust and there's a NT information centre.

Surf's up!

"I think the most important things you need to be a surfer in Wales is that you have to be very keen to deal with the cold, the wind and the pollution. And you need a good sense of humour! But on the plus side, you get to share the ocean with Welsh people." Carwyn Williams, former World Tour surfer and Welshman.

The Gower Peninsula is the surfing heartland of Wales, a series of sandy bays with reefs and points that provide no end of surfing possibilities. Some recommended places include Three Cliffs Bay, one of the most scenic beaches on the Gower and usually an uncrowded spot; Oxwich Bay, which can get busy and tends to be best at high tide, and Llangennith beach, with three miles of sand and a very good place for beginners, with a surf shop, campsite and parking nearby. More experienced surfers might like to head for Pete's Reef which can get very crowded and holds up to 5 ft, a favourite with locals.

From *Footprint Surfing Europe*, by Chris Nelson and Demi Taylor (2004).

You can walk from here to the 'humped and serpentine body' of Worm's Head rocks, home to seals and seabirds (check tide times first!), or along the glorious beach where you can sometimes see the wreck of the *Helvetia*, which went down in 1887. On fine days the sunsets here can be superb – well worth the trip to the Gower alone.

King Arthur's Stone sits inland, near **Reynoldston**. It's a massive dolmen which sits alone on a windy ridge. A giant capstone weighing around 25 tons, balanced on smaller rocks, it marks a Neolithic, communal burial chamber. The views from this isolated spot seem to stretch forever.

Carmarthen (Caerfyrddin) and around

Carmarthen is typically Welsh and the language is widely spoken here. Often regarded as the gateway to West Wales, the town on the River Tywi (also known by its anglicised name, Towy) is the ancient capital of the region. Although it was founded as a Roman fort, legend claims that it is the birthplace of Merlin (Myrddin). Once a busy trading port and wool town, Carmarthen's a flourishing market town and stronghold of the Welsh language.

▸▸ *See Sleeping p110, Eating and drinking p134*

 ## Sights

Carmarthenshire County Museum

Bishop's Palace, Abergwilli, **T** 01267 231691. *Mon-Sat 1000-1630. Free. Off the A40.*

Two miles east of Carmarthen, the former seat of the Bishop of St David's houses the regional history museum. Eclectic exhibition covering local castles, pottery, archaeological finds, and the origins of one of Wales' first eisteddfodau (Welsh cultural festivals), held nearby in 1450.

Middleton Garden (National Botanic Garden of Wales)

Llanarthne, **T** 01558 668768, www.middletongardens.com www.gardenofwales.org.uk *Daily, summer 1000-1800, winter 1000-1630. £7 adult, £2 child, £16 family, children free at weekends. Follow brown signs off the A48.*

Opened in May 2000 this is one of Wales' flagship millennium projects – its own botanic garden. The old **double walled garden** (cleverly designed so as to produce more heat) has been restored, and there's an excellent exhibition on the **Physicians** of Myddfai – a line of Welsh physicians – and a 19th-century apothecary's hall from Anglesey, complete with bottles with labels like 'Dr Rooke's Solar Elixir and Reanimating Balm of Life'. At the heart of the garden is the **Great Glasshouse** designed by Norman Foster.

Aberglasney Gardens

Llangathen, **T** 01558 668998, www.aberglasney.org.uk *Daily, summer 1000-1800, winter 1030-1600, (last entry 1 hour before closing). £5.50, £2.50 child, £14 family. Off A40 near Llandeilo.*

East of Middleton is Wales' answer to Heligan – a lost garden surrounding a fine manor house. Both the house and the weed-choked grounds were saved in the mid 1990s and a unique garden was discovered – now carefully restored. The formal **Cloister Gardens** are a rare and authentic Jacobean survival: almost all such gardens were swept away in the 18th century. There's a good café where you can sit outside on fine days.

Dinefwr Castle and Park and Newton House

Near Llandeilo, **T** 01558 823902. *House and park Apr-Oct Thu-Mon 1100-1700. £3.50, £1.70 child, £8.30 family, park only £2.30, £1.20 child, £5.80 family; unrestricted access to castle. 1 mile west of Llandeilo, off the A40.*

Legend has it that the first **castle** at Dinefwr was built in 877 AD by Rhodri Mawr, King of Wales. It became the principal court of Hywel Dda (the 'Good') who in 920 AD ruled much of South West Wales, known as Deheubarth. He was responsible for creating the first uniform legal system in Wales.

! Merlin the magician is said to sleep under a hill near Abergwili. It's called Brynn Myrddin in Welsh – that's plain old Merlin's Hill in English.

★ **Best**

Things to do outdoors

- Surf in the Gower, p71
- Watch the sunset off Rhossili, p72
- Think great thoughts by the estuary at Laugharne, p79
- Walk along the river by Tintern Abbey, p83
- Walk in the Brecon Beacons, p113

In the 17th century the more comfortable **Newton House** was built (about a 25-minute walk across parkland from the castle), and the park was landscaped in the 1770s by Capability Brown. You can see indigenous, rare White Park cattle: white with long horns and black noses. They have a lineage stretching back to the time of Hywel Dda – in the event of any injury to the King of Deheubarth tribute had to be paid in the form of these cattle

Carreg Cennen Castle

Southeast of Llandeilo, near Trapp, **T** 01558 822291. *Apr-Oct 0930-1730 daily, Nov-end Mar 0930-dusk daily. £3, £2.50 child, £8.50 family, CADW. 2 miles southeast of Llandeilo, off the A483.*

Probably the most dramatically situated castle in Wales, Carreg Cennen sits high on a precipitous crag above the River Cennen. The views down the valley are stunning. Legend has it that a castle was built here by King Arthur's knights – and one of them is still said to sleep under the existing structure, a seemingly impenetrable stone stronghold which dates from around 1300 and became a stronghold of the Welsh. It is now a romantic ruin. A visit includes taking a torch and walking along the dark passageway that leads to a cave beneath the fort.

Here the spirit of ancient Wales fills the air. I feel it every time. I can never visit Carreg Cennen Castle without experiencing a surge of emotion.

Huw Edwards, BBC Broadcaster.

The Carmarthen coast

The coastline has a completely different character to the interior and is notable as the final home of Dylan Thomas, who spent his last years in the simple boathouse at Laugharne, overlooking the 'heron-priested' shores of the sleepy estuary. Most of his greatest works, including, most famously, his 'play for voices' Under Milk Wood, were written and inspired by this little chunk of Wales, and if you're a fan of his work – or want to learn more about it – then this is the place to come.

▶▶ *See Sleeping p110, Eating and drinking p135*

 Sights

National Wetlands Centre

Penclacwydd, Llwynhendy, near Llanelli, **T** 01554 741087, www.wwt.org.uk *Daily, 0930-1700 summer, 0930-1630 winter. £5.50, £3.50 child, £14.50 family. Located west from the Gower along the A484 over the Loughor estuary.*

This is twitcher heaven, but you don't have to be a biro-clutching beardie to enjoy a visit. Five hundred pancake-flat acres around the Burry Inlet, with salt marshes and mudflats. Hides give you the opportunity to see a wide range of wildfowl and wading birds – in winter around 50,000 birds come here. There's also a good interactive **Discovery Centre** for kids, and a café.

Kidwelly Castle

Near Lllanelli, **T** 01554 890104. *Daily, 0930-1700 Apr, May end Sept-end Oct, 0930-1800 Jun-end Sept, Mon-Sat 0930-1600, Sun 1100-1600 end Oct-end Mar. £2.50, £2 concession, £7 family, CADW. West of the National Wetlands Centre, just off the A484.*

One of Wales' lesser-known castles, but it's well preserved so worth a look for anyone on the castle trail. Founded by the

What Dylan Thomas said

"We sank to the ground, the rubbery, gull-limed grass, the sheep-pilled stones, the pieces of bones and feathers, and crouched at the extreme end of the Peninsula." At Rhossili. "Ugly, lovely town, crawling, sprawling, slummed, unplanned, jerry-villa'd, and smug suburbaned by the side of a long and splendid curving shore." On Swansea. "This timeless, beautiful, barmy (both spellings) town… a legendary lazy little black magical bedlam by the sea." On Laugharne.

Normans, it was a link in a chain of coastal strongholds. Its most prominent feature is the great gatehouse, completed in 1422 – you can see the arches through which rocks were chucked on to unfortunate assailants.

Laugharne (Talacharn)

The undoubted high point of the Carmarthenshire coast is Laugharne, a must for Dylan Thomas pilgrims and the most likely inspiration for fictional Llareggub of *Under Milk Wood* which he wrote here. It's a glorious shimmery spot on the Taf Estuary, and the place that you can most easily feel the spirit of this most quotable of poets. He came here several times – once to chase after Caitlin, whom he later married – and lived in several houses around the town until in 1949 his benefactor, Margaret Taylor, bought him and his family the famous Boathouse where he lived until his death in 1953.

⬤ *A short drive inland from Laugharne is the village of **St Clears**. There's nothing much to see, but it's got a good craft centre and excellent contemporary café (see eating).*

★ Dylan Thomas Boathouse

Dylan's Walk, Laugharne, **T** 01994 427420, www.dylanthomas boathouse.com *Daily, May-Oct 1000-1700, Nov-Apr 1030-1500. £3, £1.50 child, £7 family. Best reached by car, otherwise a bus runs every 2 hrs from Carmarthen. Then walk from the carpark.*

This simple building with an idyllic location is perched on the clifftop with glorious views over the estuary and its 'heron-priested shores'. It's reached by a narrow track from the town (and is so poorly signposted that you're sure to miss it at first). The tiny writing shed is laid out much as it was when Thomas worked here, with scrunched up pieces of paper on the floor and a bottle of beer on the table. Downstairs in the house itself is the simply furnished living room, with some copies of his manuscripts and other memorabilia, and upstairs there's a video presentation. Nearby, in the village, is **St Martin's Churchyard**, where Thomas and his wife are buried.

Laugharne Castle

T 01994 427906. *Daily, Apr-Sep 1000-1700. £2.75, £2.25 concession, £7.75 family. By the estuary car park in Laugharne.*

Close to the Boathouse, on the shore is this atmospheric ruin built in the mid to late 13th century. In Elizabethan times it was turned into a mansion but after the Civil War fell into decline. JMW Turner painted it and Dylan Thomas sometimes worked in its summerhouse.

! Dylan Thomas was having a sly joke when he came up with the name Llareggub for the fictional town in *Under Milk Wood*. Say it backwards and you'll see why.

Monmouthshire

When George Borrow wrote his famous travelogue 'Wild Wales',
Monmouthshire was considered to be English rather than Welsh.
Although now officially part of Wales, the county still feels less
immediately Welsh than the borderlands further north. Once it was
the scene of fierce fighting, as locals resisted first Roman and then
Norman incursions on their land. There are vivid reminders of those
times in the extensive Roman remains at Caerleon and the 'don't mess
with me' Norman castle at Chepstow. The west of the county,
particularly around the city of Newport, is industrialised, but becomes
increasingly green as you move east. There are good golf courses here
– in 2010 the Ryder Cup is coming to Newport. The most beautiful
area is the lush, green Wye Valley: an area of Outstanding Natural
Beauty formed as the River Wye ripples along the border from
Monmouth to Chepstow. The valley, an excellent area for walking and
canoeing, is home to one of the most celebrated sites in Wales –
Tintern Abbey, a picturesque ruin, right on the border with England.

▶▶ *See Sleeping p111, Eating and drinking p136*

Sights

Newport Transporter Bridge

This unusual 19th century bridge was built by a Frenchman and
enabled road traffic to pass from one quay to another – better
than a hazardous ferry trip on a stretch of water that has one of
the highest tides in the world. Cars sit on a platform which then
glides across the water.

Chepstow Castle

Off Bridge St, **T** 01291 624065. *Apr, May, end Sep-late Oct , 0930-1700 daily, Jun-end Sep 0930-1800 daily; late Oct-end Mar 0930-1600 Mon-Sat, 1100-1600 Sun, last entry 30 mins prior to closing. £3, £2.50 children, £8.50 family, CADW.*

This, the first stone castle built in Britain, occupies a superb position on a bend of the Wye, with wonderful views along the river as you wander round the ruins. More than a little battle-scarred, Chepstow castle was a significant stronghold and the base for many English raids and attacks on Wales. The oldest part of the castle is the **Great Tower**, dating back to 1067. The **Great Hall**, also dating back to 1067, is of particular historic significance, as the oldest surviving stone fortification in Britain.

Chepstow Museum

Bridge St, near the castle, **T** 01291 625981. *Summer Mon-Sat 1030-1730, Sun 1400-1730, winter Mon-Sat 1100-1700, 1400-1700 Sun. Free.*

Chepstow Museum has displays on the town and local history, including the story of local man Able Seaman Williams who won the VC at Gallipoli, and information on the growth and development of the former port and market town. Upstairs is a room containing a variety of old machines, including a 'permanent waving machine' c.1940 that bears a strong resemblance to an instrument of torture. There's also a collection of 19th- and 20th-century prints and drawings of Chepstow and the surrounding area.

Abbey fashionable
Tintern Abbey has inspired great poets and artists and today attracts visitors by the coachload.

★ Tintern Abbey

Tintern, by the A466, **T** 01291 689251. *1 Apr-1 June, 29 Sept-26 Oct 0930-1700 daily; 2 June-28 Sept 0930-1800 daily, 27 Oct -31 Mar 0930-1600 Mon-Sat, 1100-1600 Sun, last admission 30 mins prior to closing. £3, £2.50 concession, £8.50 family, CADW. Take bus 69 to reach Tintern from Chepstow.*

Founded in 1131 for Cistercian monks – known as the 'white monks' for the colour of their habits – the abbey became increasingly wealthy and its power was reflected in a grand rebuilding programme in the late 13th century. It flourished until dissolution in 1536, then gained a new lease of life as a romantic ruin in the 18th century, its picturesque beauty and glorious setting inspiring both Wordsworth and JMW Turner. The abbey, a beautiful shell, with soaring archways, and delicate stonework, still

Notes from a river walk

'I picked up a riverside path by the town's handsome stone bridge and followed it north along the Welsh bank… at a place called Goldsmith's Wood the river bent sharply away from the road and I was suddenly in another, infinitely more tranquil world. Birds fussed and twittered in the trees above and small, unseen creatures plinked into the water at my approach.' Bill Bryson, *Notes from a Small Island*, describing a walk along the Wye from Monmouth .

attracts bus loads of tourists today, so try to visit early in the morning or late in the day. To really see the ruins at their best you should cross the Wye at a nearby bridge and follow the path to view the abbey from the opposite bank.

A mile from the abbey is **Tintern Old Station** (**T** 01291 689566, *daily Apr-Oct 1030-1730*), a Victorian station now converted into a visitor and information centre, with a camping area nearby.

Monmouth/Trefynwy

North of Tintern, where the Wye joins the Monnow, is the handsome town of Monmouth. The heart of the town is **Agincourt Square**, a reminder that Henry V was born here and won the Battle of Agincourt (1415) with the help of Welsh archers. There's a statue here of **Charles Rolls** of Rolls Royce fame – holding a model of an aircraft. He was also a pioneer aviator and in 1910 became the first person to make a double crossing of the Channel. A month later he was killed when his plane crashed at an airshow.

Nelson Museum and Local History Centre
Priory St, **T** 01600 710630. *1000-1300, 1400-1700 daily, excluding Sun, 1400-1700. Free.*

Charles Rolls' mother, Lady Llangattock, was a distant relative of Lord Nelson and her collection of Nelson memorabilia is displayed here. Among the exhibits are various fake personal effects, manufactured to profit from the cult of Nelson that flourished after his death. One is a glass eye, presumably once proudly displayed in a cabinet along with the best china. However, the makers got it wrong: although Nelson was famously blind in one eye ('I see no ships'), he only lost the sight, and never the eye itself.

Monnow Bridge is a fortified medieval bridge, built in the 13th century. It's the only complete example of its kind in Britain.

Usk Rural Life Museum
New Market St, Usk, **T** 01291 673777. *Easter-end Oct, Mon-Fri 1000-1700, weekends 1400-1700. £2, £1 child. On A449 from Newport.*

Usk is a little town with several good places to eat and drink, and pretty, well cared for buildings. Its fascinating Rural Life Museum is housed in three converted barns. It focuses on rural life from 1850 to the end of the Second World War and has a vast collection of old farming implements, with ploughs, tractors, scythes and grim items like castrating irons.

Caerleon

On the outskirts of Newport, this was a Roman town – Isca – and was founded in 75 AD. It became a major base for the Roman legions – one of only three in Britain. Around 5,500 troops of the second Augustan Legion were housed here, in a sophisticated garrison complete with amphitheatre, baths (see below) and shops. The **amphitheatre** (*daily, free*), which seated 6,000 and had boxes for

VIPS, is impressive and it is not too difficult to imagine bloodthirsty contests between gladiators and wild animals. It was only excavated in the 1920s – before this it was concealed by a grassy mound, once thought to be King Arthur's Round Table. The new-agey **Ffwrrwm Centre** (*open approximately 0930-1730*), focuses on Caerleon's Arthurian links and has a courtyard filled with wooden sculptures, as well as little shops and a bistro.

Fortress Baths
T 01633 422518. *Daily 0930-1700 (last entry 1630) Apr-late Oct, Nov-end Mar 0930-1700 Mon-Sat, 1200-1700 Sun (last admin 1630), £2.50, £2 child, £7 family, CADW, buses run from Newport.*

By the Bull Hotel car park is the one-time 'leisure centre' for the Roman soldiers with a swimming pool, heated changing rooms, hot and cold baths and a gymnasium. Finds from local excavations are displayed in the **Roman Legionary Museum** (**T** 01633 423134, *daily, free*).

Caerphilly and the Valleys

Most tourists bypass the Valleys for the more conventional attractions of the beaches of the Pembrokeshire coast or the mountains of Snowdonia. Yet these distinctive communities, with their rows of terraced houses squeezed into the valleys of the mountains that lie between Cardiff and the Brecon Beacons, are full of history. These were the coal- and iron-producing heartlands of the Industrial Revolution, where close working-class communities lived harsh lives under the gloomy shadow of hills scarred and blackened with slag heaps.

When the coal-mining industry died, so to a large extent did the Valleys, with unemployment devastating the population. But the slag heaps have now gone or been greened over, some coal mines are now museums and Blaenavon, a world heritage site, is reinventing itself as a booktown. The towns are still poor, but the people very friendly; the surrounding hills are stunning and the glimpse of the industrial past is fascinating.

▸▸ *See Sleeping p112, Eating and drinking p138*

◉ Sights

Caerphilly Castle
Caerphilly, **T** 02920 883143, www.cadw.wales.gov.uk *0930-1800, Jun-Sep, 0930-1700, Apr, May, Oct, 0930- 1600, Nov-Mar, 1100-1600, Sun. £3 adult, £2.50 child, £8.50 family, CADW. Nearest station is Caerphilly or take the A469 from Cardiff.*

This vast medieval fortress, spread over 30 acres, is the second largest castle in Europe. It was built from 1268 by one of Henry III's most powerful barons, to prevent the area falling into the hands of the Welsh. The castle's so huge, the poet Tennyson wrote: 'It isn't a castle – it's a town in ruins'.

Llancaiach Fawr Manor
Nelson, Caerphilly, **T** 01443 412248. *Mar-end Oct Mon-Fri 1000-1700, Sat, Sun 1000-1800, closed Mon Nov-Feb. £4.50, £3 child, £12 family. On B4254 near Nelson, north of Caerphilly.*

This lovely old manor house was built in 1530 and is now a living history museum. It focuses on the year 1645 – the Civil War – when then owner Col Edward Prichard changed his allegiance from the Royalist to the Parliamentarian cause. The informative guides are dressed in period costume and speak and act as they would have in the 17th century (it works well – honest). The rooms have been restored and furnished to the period and there are also 17th-century style gardens.

Castell Coch

West of Caerphilly, **T** 02920 810101. *Jun-end Sep daily 0930-1800, Apr-Jun, Oct 0930-1700, Nov-Mar 0930-1600 Mon-Sat, 1100-1600 Sun. £3, £2.50 child, £8.50 family, CADW. Off the A470, 5 miles northwest of Cardiff.*

Like Cardiff Castle, the lavishly eccentric interiors of this castle are a result of the partnership of the Marquess of Bute and architect William Burges. Their joint love of gothic fantasy and Bute's vast fortune allowed them to create extravagant rooms, complete with gilded ceilings, walls painted with golden apples, monkeys and peacocks, and elaborate furniture and fittings. You half expect to see Rapunzel letting down her hair from one of the turrets' windows.

Blaenavon Ironworks

North St, **T** 01495 792615, www.blaenavontic.com *Apr-end Oct, Mon-Fri 0930-1630, Sat 1000-1700, Sun 1000-1630, last entry 30 mins prior to closing. £2, £1.50 concession, £5.50 family, pre book for guided tours' minimum price £25.*

In 2000 the industrial town of Blaenavon/Blaenafon was designated a UNESCO World Heritage Site, a recognition of the important role it played in the Industrial Revolution. The town's 18th century ironworks are some of the best preserved in Europe and they make an impressive sight. Established in 1788 – the site being chosen for its abundance of coal, iron-ore, limestone and water – they were at the cutting edge of technology, using steam rather than water to power the furnaces. By 1796 Blaenavon was the second largest producer of iron in Wales. In later years the metallurgist Sidney Gilchrist Thomas worked from here, spawning the mighty steel industry. As well as the remains of the works, there's a little terrace of iron-workers cottages – inhabited until 1973.

Best

★ **Buildings**

- The wacky interior at Cardiff Castle, p33
- The snowy white City Hall, p46
- Dylan Thomas' little boathouse, p80
- The romantic ruins of Tintern Abbey, p83
- The equally wacky interior at Castell Coch, p88

● *Blaenavon is now in the process of reinventing itself as a **book town** (www.booktownblaenafon.com), on the same lines as Hay-on-Wye. To date 11 book shops have opened, selling everything from cookery books to travel titles.*

★ Big Pit National Mining Museum

About 1 mile west of Blaenavon, **T** 01495 790311, www.nmgw.ac.uk *Mid Feb-end Nov daily 0930-1700, first tour 1000, last 1530. Free.*

High on the moors is this former coal mine gives an excellent insight into the life of the Valleys' miners. Coal was mined from 1880 until 1980 – the site opening as a museum in 1983. In its heyday it employed 1,300 men and produced more than 250,000 tons of coal a year. The highlight of a visit is the tour, which takes you 3,000 ft (90 m) **underground**. You don a helmet, cap-lamp and battery pack and, guided by ex-miners, go down to the coal face where you see the miserable conditions under which people worked. Not just people either – the underground stables still bear the names of the pit ponies who spent their lives in darkness. The last ponies around here were only brought to the surface in 1972. You can also see the listed 1930s **Pithead Baths**, and a multi-media presentation covering the history of coal mining. There's a pleasant little café too.

Merthyr Tydfil (Merthyr Tudful)

The name of Merthyr Tydfil is synonymous with the industrial past. In the 18th century its rich supplies of iron ore and limestone were discovered and exploited. It became the most important iron-producing town in the world. The population swelled rapidly as workers swarmed in – being housed as cheaply as possible by their wealthy masters. The appalling working conditions and poor cramped housing led to a wave of radicalism: in 1831 there was a violent workers uprising (when the Red Flag – which had been dipped in a calf's blood – was raised for the first time) and in 1900 it became the first town in Britain to elect a Socialist MP, Keir Hardie. When the industry declined in the 20th century Merthyr suffered terribly from the consequent depression.

Joseph Parry's Cottage, at 4 Chapel Row, (**T** 01685 721858, *Apr-Sep Thu-Sun 1400-1700, free*), is a preserved iron-worker's cottage, part of a terrace built in 1825 for skilled workers employed in the Cyfartha Ironworks. The ground floor rooms are furnished simply, as they would have been in the 1840s. Upstairs there's an exhibition about composer Joseph Parry who was born here and wrote the Welsh tune *Myfanwy*.

In lavish contrast to the cottage, **Cyfartha Castle** on Brecon Rd, (**T** 01685 723112, *daily, Apr-Sep 1000-1730, Oct-Mar 1000-1600 Tue-Fri, 1200-1600 Sat, Sun, free*) was built at a cost of £30,000 in 1825 by the Crawshay family, who owned the Cyfartha Ironworks. There are displays on singer Paul Robeson, who had strong links with the miners and raised money for them in 1929. There's a good collection of local Nantgarw ware, displays on Male Voice Choirs, the Iron Industry, Welsh Nationalism and the miners strike of 1984-85. You can also see paintings by artists such as Jack Butler Yeats (brother of the famous poet), Kyffin Williams, Cedric Morris – and George Frederick Harris, Rolf Harris' grandfather, who was born in Merthyr. There's a good value café here too.

Near Merthyr Tydfil is Pant Station where the **Brecon Mountain Railway**, a narrow-gauge steam railway, takes you into the National Park (**T** 01685 722988, www.breconmountain railway.co.uk, *Easter-end Oct, generally closed Mon and Fri Mar-May and Sept, Oct. £7.50, £3.75 child, family ticket available*). Pant Station is signposted off the A470, or take bus 35 from Merthyr bus station.

Rhondda Heritage Park

Coed Cae Rd, Trehafod, **T** 01443 682036, www.rhonddaheritagepark.com *Daily 1000-1800, last tour 1600, closed Mon Oct-Easter. £5.60 adult, £4.30 children, £16.50 family. Trains run from Cardiff to Trehafod from where it's a 10-min walk.*

Based at the former Lewis Merthyr Colliery, there's an interesting exhibition looking at life in the valleys, with recreated shops and house interiors. Panels tell the story of the colliery and the appalling Tynewydd Colliery disaster in 1877 when the pit was flooded and many men trapped underground. Tours of the site are available and there's also a good selection of books on life in the Valleys.

Margam Stones Museum

Near Port Talbot, **T** 02920 500200. *Wed-Sun 1000-1600. £2 adults, £1.50 children, £5.50 family. 4 miles southeast of Port Talbot, off A48.*

A fine collection of early-Christian sculptured stones. The Bodvoc Stone once sat on Margam mountain set into a line of prehistoric barrows; 10th- and 11th-century crosses found at a nearby farm; and a 6th-century memorial stone to Pumpeius Carantorius, with Ogham inscriptions which look rather like Morse code. The nearby church is well worth a visit, containing 16th- and 17th-century tombs.

Margam Park

Near Port Talbot, **T** 01639 881635, www.neath-porttalbot.gov.uk/
margampark *Daily, Easter-end Sep 1000-1730, winter 1000-1630.
Free, £2 car park. Reached by junction 38, M4.*

Delightful parkland surrounding an elaborate 19th-century house
and the romantic ruins of **Margam Abbey**. In the gardens is an
elegant 18th-century **Orangery**, a walled garden, fuchsia
collections, play area for children – and contemporary artworks by
artists such as Paul Williams and Elizabeth Frink.

 # Brecon Beacons National Park

*Covering 520 square miles of wild countryside in south Wales, the
Brecon Beacons National Park is a magnet for lovers of the
outdoors. While none of the mountains is over that magical 3,000 ft,
this still isn't 'walking for softies' country and the terrain can be
rugged and windswept: it's not for nothing that the SAS train here,
sending hopefuls up and down the highest peak, Pen-y-fan (2,907 ft,
886 m), in order to wear them down both physically and mentally.
The wildest part of the National Park is in the west where **Fforest
Fawr**, a former hunting forest, now an area of lonely uplands and
waterfalls, leads to the bleak and barren expanse of **Black
Mountain** – the least-visited area with the most challenging walks.
The central area is occupied by the eponymous **Brecon Beacons**
range, to the north of which is the busy town of **Brecon**, a popular
base for a wide range of outdoor activities. The Monmouthshire and
Brecon Canal offers some undemanding walks, before the National
Park stretches out to the edge of **Abergavenny**, and the famous
book town of **Hay-on-Wye**, both of which are great bases for
exploring the brooding **Black Mountains** in the east.*

»» *See Sleeping p113, Eating and drinking p138*

◉ Sights

Western Brecon Beacons

The Black Mountains and Fforest Fawr are noted for their wild, unspoilt landscapes. The main visitor attraction – and a good place to take kids on a rainy day – are the **Dan-yr-Ogof Showcaves**, off the A4067 (**T** 01639 730801, www.showcaves.co.uk, daily, Apr-Oct 1000-around 1600, varies with season, £8.80 adult, £5.80 child). Discovered in 1912 by two local farmers, the three caves contain stalactites, waterfalls and exhibits on Bronze-Age and Iron-Age life aimed at kids. There's also a **dinosaur park** and **dry ski slope**.

Brecon (Aberhonddu)

The undoubted hub of the National Park, this solid market town tends to be peopled by local farmers and visiting walkers. The highest peak in the National Park, Pen-y-Fan, can be reached easily from here, as can the **Brecon Beacons Mountain Centre** and the indoor climbing centre at **Llangorse** (see activities). The town is the northern end of the **Monmouthshire and Brecon canal**, and you can take trips along the waters (see activities).

In 1093 a Benedictine Priory was established here, and you can still see the Norman font in **Brecon Cathedral** (T 01874 625222, *daily 0830-1800, free*), on Priory Hill. In the 15th century it became a focus of pilgrimage, as the central crucifix in the rood screen (destroyed during the Reformation) was believed to have healing properties. After the dissolution of the monasteries the building became a Parish church, and was made the cathedral in 1923. After you've wandered round the cathedral you can visit the small **Heritage Centre** (*Mar-Dec, Mon-Sat 1030-1630, Sun 1200-1500, free*) which has exhibits on the cathedral.

The **Oriel Jazz Gallery**, The Watton, (**T** *01874 625557, Mon-Sat 1100-1700, and Sun in summer*), looks at the development of jazz – and the town's thriving annual Jazz Festival.

Anyone who's a fan of the film *Zulu* (1964) should head for the **South Wales Borderers' Museum**, The Watton (**T** *01874 623111, Apr-Sep 0900-1700 daily, Oct-end Mar 0900-1700 Mon-Fri, £3, under 16 free*) which tells the story of the regiment that fought at Rorke's Drift in 1879.

Crickhowell (Crug Hywel)

With plenty of places to eat, drink and sleep, the pretty little town of Crickhowell is an excellent base for exploring the eastern Brecon Beacons. Once an important stop for stagecoaches, the town is squeezed between Usk and Table Mountain. It's a great place for walkers, with a choice of routes going up **Table Mountain**, along the river, or into the **Black Mountains** to the east. It's also easy to arrange activities such as paragliding, canoeing and caving if you're one for a bit of an adrenaline rush.

Tretower (Tre-twr)
Tretower, **T** 01874 730279. *Mar-Oct daily 1000-1630. £2.50, £2 concession, £7 family. CADW. 3 miles north of town.*

The first settlement here was a Norman earthwork castle, built around 1100 to guard an important route through the Black Mountains. The house is a fine late-medieval home with a galleried courtyard and well-preserved **Great Hall**, with a huge hearth and high ceiling. The old kitchen contains displays of various herbs commonly used in medieval times – including dandelion, nettle, sage and sorrel. The main bedchamber is thought to have had a secret opening in the wood panelling so that the occupant could keep a close eye on events in the Great Hall below.

Abergavenny (Y Fenni)

Just on the edge of the National Park, Abergavenny is surrounded by delightful countryside and makes an excellent base for exploring and walking. Perhaps its most famous resident was Hitler's deputy, Rudolf Hess, who was imprisoned at **Maindiss Court** near the town after the plane in which he was flying crashed in Scotland in 1941. He was allowed out once a week for walks in the hills – and became a regular at one of the local pubs.

The **castle** is now ruined but was the scene of an infamous massacre at Christmas in 1175 when the Norman lord, William de Braose, avenging the killing of his uncle by the Welsh, invited local Welsh chieftains to join him at a banquet – and then murdered them. Around Abergavenny are the hills of **Blorenge** (1,834 ft) to the south west – a favourite with paragliders and hang gliders, and burial place of Col Llewellyn's famous champion horse Foxhunter; **Skirrid-Fawr** (1,596 ft/486 m) in the northeast, and **Sugar Loaf** (1,955 ft, 596 m) in the northwest.

From Abergavenny there is a wonderful **scenic drive** to the famous Welsh booktown of Hay-on-Wye, an effortless way of enjoying the striking beauty of the Black Mountains. You can pick up the road at Llanfihangel Crucorney, north of the town, and then follow the unclassified road as it leads you to Llanthony Priory, then on to the hamlet of Capel-y-Ffin, past the viewpoint at Hay Bluff and down into Hay-on-Wye. Be aware that the road is a single track for much of the way.

Llanthony Priory

Now a picturesque and sleepy ruin, Llanthony was founded in 1108, probably on the site of a sixth-century hermitage. The medieval traveller Giraldus Cambrensis described it as 'truly calculated for religion' and the description still holds true today. There is a sense of peace and spirituality here that is missing from better known and more commercialised sites, such as Tintern Abbey.

★ Hay-on-Wye (Y Gelli)

From a lone second-hand bookshop in 1961, Hay-on-Wye now has over 30, specialising in everything from apiculture to erotica – the town is bliss for bibliophiles. The former cinema alone has a stock of around 200,000 books and every other building in town, including the old castle, seems to be filled with wonderful piles of dusty tomes, old school annuals and rare first editions. The widest selection of all is at **Richard Booth's Bookshop**, Lion Street, with over 400,000 titles for sale. Booth was the force behind Hay's rejuvenation as a booktown, opening the first secondhand bookshop here and promoting Hay to the extent that it is now known throughout the world as a centre for secondhand books. In 1977, on 1 April, Booth declared Hay, right on the border of England and Wales, an independent state – proclaiming himself king in the process. The town is busiest during the annual Hay Festival, an excellent literary festival that attracts the biggest names in literature.

There's an increasing variety of places to stay in Cardiff and the trend looks to continue as the city grows. Most places are located in the city centre where there are several well-established, traditional hotels and a clutch of newer chains, which offer reliable and comfortable accommodation. There are also some funkier places to kip, aimed very much at 20- and 30-something travellers. Cardiff Bay has less choice but there are a number of places opening up. It's also the place to find the city's swishest hotel, a five-star hotel and spa, offering a chance to indulge in some luxurious living. Most of the city-centre hotels will offer good deals during the low season (though never on big match weekends) and prices can vary enormously, so it's always worth ringing around and asking what they can do. Many of the smaller hotels, guesthouses and B&Bs are concentrated on Cathedral Road to the west of the city centre, while there are some others along the busy Newport Road to the east. At the lower end of the scale there are a couple of hostels, and the university also offers campus accommodation.

Sleeping codes

Price			
L	£160 and over	D	£30-50
A	£100-160	E	£15-30
B	£80-100	F	£15 and under
C	£50-80		

Prices are per night for a double room in high season

City Centre

Hotels

L Angel Hotel, Castle St, **T** 02920 649200,
www.paramount-hotels.co.uk *Map 2, E5, p238* 102 rooms. This
reliable Victorian hotel is sandwiched between Cardiff Castle and
the Millennium Stadium. A mere Gareth Edwards sidestep from
the shops, it is a perennial favourite with locals and regular
visitors. They've got a restaurant serving traditional British food
and afternoon teas. If you pop into the ground floor bar for a
quiet drink on a Saturday afternoon, you may find yourself as an
extra at the wedding of one of Cardiff's finest.

A Hilton Hotel, Kingsway, **T** 02920 646300, www.hilton.com
Map 2, E7, p238 Elegant and tasteful, this hotel attracts the great
and the good (and its fair share of star guests) thanks to its fab
location looking over to the creamy-stoned Civic Centre and
Cardiff Castle. They've got a Health Club with a 20-m
stainless-steel pool and a well-equipped gym, sauna and spa. The
upmarket bar and restaurant attract a mixed crowd of visiting
business people, well-heeled tourists and smart locals thanks to
its reputation for discreet service.

A Holland House Hotel, 24-26 Newport Rd, **T** 0870 1220020, www.macdonaldhollandhouse.co.uk *Map 2, F12, p238* 165 rooms. This large new four-star chain opened in Spring 2004. It caters mainly for the business and conference market and also has a spa with treatment rooms, 18 m swimming pool, sauna and steam room.

A Marriott Hotel, Mill Lane, **T** 02920 399944, **F** 02920 392278, www.marriott.com *Map 2, H7, p238* 182 rooms. Standing cheek by jowl with Cardiff's Café Quarter, this four-star hotel claims to be Cardiff's premier hotel and offers the standard facilities you'd expect of a major chain, though the exterior is less than enticing. Not funky but reliable. There's a gym, sauna and solarium, and a restaurant serving Mediterranean food.

B Thistle Hotel, Park Place, **T** 02920 383471, 0870 3339257, **F** 02920 39777, www.thistlehotels.com/cardiff *Map 2, E9, p238* 136 rooms. Confident Victorian building, with rooms decorated in trad style with comfy furnishings and swagged curtains, this hotel's location in the heart of the pedestrianised zone makes it handy for shopping and schlepping around town.

C Big Sleep Hotel, Bute Terrace, **T** 02920 636363, www.thebigsleephotel.com *Map 2, H9, p238* 81 rooms. Listed as one of the best budget boutique hotels in the world and co-owned by John Malkovich, this high rise is chic and comfortable, with chilled rooms offering views right across the city. Breakfast is a continental buffet with do-it-yourself toast, cereals and little pastries. Style on a budget and very popular with a younger crowd. Parking.

C Cathedral Hotel, 53 Cathedral Rd, **T** 02920 236511, **F** 02920 225157, www.cathedral-hotel.com *Map 2, C2, p238* 40 rooms. This is a family-run hotel on a tree-lined road out to the leafy suburb of Pontcanna, but 10 minute's walk from the city centre. Facilities include a gym, bar, restaurant and parking.

C Sandringham Hotel, 21 St Mary St, **T** 02920 232161, **F** 02920 383998, www.sandringham-hotel.com *Map 2, G6, p238* 28 rooms. This may not be in the most peaceful location in town, but if you want somewhere central and handily-placed for the Millennium Stadium, then this bustling family-run hotel will float your boat. The jazz café adds to the ambience.

D Ibis Hotel, Churchill Way, **T** 02920 649250, www.ibishotel.com *Map 2, G10, p238* 102 rooms. Located close to Cardiff International Arena, these small but modern and functional en suite rooms are rather sterile, but the central location and friendly welcome more than compensate.

Guesthouses and B&Bs

C Beaufort Guest House, 65 Cathedral Rd, **T** 02920 237003, **F** 02920 407235, www.beauforthousecardiff.co.uk *Map 2, B2, p238* Nine rooms. About 10 minutes' walk from the castle, this guesthouse is in a large Victorian semi that's recently been refurbished. All the rooms are en suite and each is slightly different. Private car parking.

Hostels

D-F Cardiff Backpackers, 98 Neville St, Riverside, **T** 02920 345577, www.cardiffbackpackers.com *5 mins walks from Cardiff Central. Map 2, E2, p238* Funky and friendly hostel accommodation about half a mile from Cardiff Central station. Cheerful single, double, triple and bunk bedroom options are available. The bright and welcoming communal areas include café-style chairs and tables, a fully licensed bar and great squashy sofas.

Cardiff Bay

Hotels

L St David's Hotel and Spa, Havannah Street, Cardiff Bay, **T** 02920 454045, **F** 02920 313075, www.rfhotels.com *Map 3, H1, p240* 132 rooms. Local wags would have you believe that the rf stands for 'really fancy', but it is Rocco Forte's luxurious waterfront hotel which dominates the Bay's skyline. Decor is contemporary and all rooms have balconies. The swish spa offers all kinds of treatments and has a swimming pool, fitness centre and solarium. The restaurant menus were created by Marco Pierre White – though don't expect to find Marco toiling away in the kitchen or throwing a trademark tantrum. Parking is available but costs £4.20 for 24 hours.

B-A Jolyon's, 5 Bute Crescent, Cardiff Bay, **T** 07815 125130, www.jolyons.com *Map 3, F3, p240* Six rooms. This non-smoking boutique hotel is due to open in late summer 2004. The rooms will all be individually designed – one will have a verandah, another a four-poster bed. Furniture has been imported from Holland and France and there'll be Welsh slate in the bathrooms. There will be free use of the internet and you can arrange to be picked up from the airport. The owner says that vegetarians, vegans and those with special diets will all be catered for – while anyone wanting a kick start to the day should ask for porridge, as they're promising to add a generous dash of Welsh whisky to it.

C Express by Holiday Inn Hotel, Longueil Close, Schooner Way, Cardiff Bay, **T** 02920 449000, www.exhicardiff.co.uk *Map 3, C4, p240* 87 rooms. Less pricey (and less luxurious) than St David's, the modern, functional rooms are ideal if you are looking for easy access to the Bay and want to spend your time out and about. Good access from the M4 makes it a popular stopover for business travellers.

City suburbs

Guesthouses and B&Bs

C **The Old Post Office**, Greenwood Lane, St Fagans, **T** 02920 565400, www.old-post-office.com *Map 1, C1, p236* Six rooms. Situated a few miles outside Cardiff, opposite the Museum of Welsh Life in the village of St Fagans, this former post office and police station has been converted into a restaurant with rooms. Decor is clean, crisp and modern; all the rooms are en suite and there's a little garden. Very popular with couples who want to treat themselves.

C **Penrhys Hotel**, 127 Cathedral Road, Pontcanna, **T** 02920 230548. *Map 1, C7, p236* 20 rooms. Family-run hotel offering en suite rooms with TV. The Victorian building boasts a splendid tower and dining room complete with beautiful stained glass and dark wood.

C-D **Church Hotel**, 126 Cathedral Rd, Pontcanna, **T** 02920 340881. *Map 1, C7, p236* Nine rooms. Vegetarian-friendly accommodation in large Victorian house, recently taken over by Charlotte Church's parents. Most rooms en suite with colour TV, but no off-road parking available. There are three family rooms sleeping up to four people. Vegetarian breakfasts by advance request. Don't expect to see Charlotte serving the toast though.

C-D **Courtfield Hotel**, 101 Cathedral Rd, Pontcanna, **T/F** 02920 227701, www.courtfieldhotel.com *Map 1, C7, p236* Eight rooms. Well-run B&B set up in 1950 and still going strong. Some en suite rooms, off-street parking and a licensed bar – handy before a day's rugby-watching or after a hard day hitting the shops.

D Anedd Lon, 157 Cathedral Rd, **T** 02920 223349, **F** 02920 6440885. *Map 1, C7, p236* Six rooms. Pretty hanging baskets welcome you to this comfortable, family-run B&B offering no-smoking, en suite accommodation in sedate Pontcanna. Reasonably convenient for city centre and off-street parking to the rear of the building.

D Maxine's, 150 Cathedral Rd, **T** 02920 220288, **F** 02920 344884. *Map 1, C7, p236* 10 rooms. Straightforward, no frills B&B in light, bright surroundings offering value for money in the leafy Pontcanna district. Handy for the smart parade of local stores further up Cathedral Rd. Not all rooms are en suite.

D Town House, 70 Cathedral Rd, Pontcanna, **T** 02920 239399, **F** 02920 223214, www.thetownhousecardiff.co.uk *Map 1, C7, p236* Eight rooms. Pleasant rooms in an imposing and recently restored three-storey Victorian townhouse. Antiques and old fireplaces in the public rooms, while breakfast is taken round one big table in the conservatory. All rooms en suite, off-road parking.

Hostels

E Cardiff Youth Hostel, 2 Wedal Rd, Roath Park, **T** 02920 462303, www.yha.org.uk *Bus 28, 29, 29B from Cardiff Central*. *Map 1, B9, p236* Handily placed near an Indian and Italian restaurant in the student district of Cathays, several bus stops and two miles north of the city centre. Popular hostel, continental breakfasts available.

Campus accommodation

E Cardiff University, Cathays, **T** 02920 875508, www.cardiff.ac.uk/resi *Locations north of the city centre*. *Map 1, A9, p236* Thousands of rooms, 50% en suite, available during vacation season (Jun-Sep) – room only, B&B, self-catering and sports facilities.

Vale of Glamorgan

Hotels

A **The Great House**, Laleston, Bridgend, **T** 01656 657644, www.great-house-laleston.co.uk. *Off A48*. 16 rooms. Reminders of old Wales in this restored 16th-century building, complete with oak beams and mullioned windows.

B **Egerton Grey Country House**, Porthkerry, Barry, **T** 01446 711666, www.egertongrey.co.uk *Jct 33 of M4, follow signs to airport then Porthkerry*. 10 en suite rooms. Plush 17th-century country house, filled with antiques, paintings, oak panelling and period detail. It's set in secluded gardens – anyone for croquet? – but is convenient for the nearby airport. They've got a restaurant serving traditional, high-quality, British fare.

C **Court Colman Manor**, Pe-y-Fai, Bridgend, **T** 01656 720212, **F** 01656 724544, www.court-colman-manor.com *2 miles off Jct 36 of M4*. 30 en suite rooms. Grand old manor house set in its own grounds, with a pleasant mixture of styles. There are open fires and comfy sofas in the wood-panelled public rooms, while the themed bedrooms have anything from traditional Indian to Moroccan styles. Simpler, more basic, rooms are also available. Their restaurant serves widely acclaimed and great-value Indian and Mediterranean food.

Guesthouses and B&Bs

C **Llanerch Vineyard**, Hensol, Pendoylan, **T** 01443 225877, **F** 01443 225546, www.llanerch-vineyard.co.uk *1 mile from Jct 34 of M4*. Nine rooms. High-quality B&B in a traditional farmhouse at Wales' best-known vineyard, 15 mins from Cardiff. There are also self-contained studio rooms in converted farm buildings.

Swansea (Abertawe) and around

Hotels

L Morgan's Hotel, Somerset Place, Swansea, **T** 01792 484848, www.morganshotel.co.uk 200 rooms. This is Catherine and Michael's hotel of choice and the place to come if you want to treat yourself. All the rooms are named after local ships and are individually designed. There are wooden floors, crisp sheets and comfy beds, and plasma TVs set into the walls. Bathrooms have scented candles and lovely big baths and there's a posh restaurant.

A Marriott Hotel, Maritime Quarter, Swansea, **T** 01792 642020/0870 4007282 www.marriott.com 122 rooms. Its location redeems the uninspiring exterior of this four-star chain hotel with small swimming pool, sauna and fitness equipment. It is well placed next to the marina and most rooms have lovely views, either of the marina or Swansea Bay. Ask for a view when you book.

B Hillcrest House Hotel, 1 Higher Lane, Langland, Mumbles, **T** 01792 363700, www.hillcresthousehotel.com This is a small, comfortable hotel with friendly owners and individually themed rooms (lots of daffodils for the Welsh room for instance, including a giant, triffid like standard lamp). All the rooms are en suite and there's private parking.

B-C Beaumont Hotel, 72-73 Walter St, Swansea, **T** 01792 643956, www.beaumonthotel.co.uk 16 rooms. Family-run two-star hotel with well-furnished and comfortable bedrooms. The executive rooms are larger and have sunken bath tubs.

C Devon View, 394-396 Oystermouth Rd, Swansea, **T** 01792 462008, www.devonview.co.uk 16 rooms, most en suite. This three-star hotel is on the seafront and some rooms have great views. It's in a Victorian terrace, and vies with the White House for best floral displays. They do a full breakfast and also have a restaurant carvery.

C **White House Hotel**, 4 Nyanza Terrace, Swansea, **T** 01792 473856, www.thewhitehousehotel.co.uk Nine rooms. This is a beautifully refurbished and maintained Victorian hotel located a mile from the city centre. The en suite rooms are comfortable and warm and the owners are friendly. They make up packed lunches if you ask, and evening meals are also available. The exterior's colourful in summer and they win Swansea in Bloom nearly every year.

C **Windsor Lodge Hotel**, Mount Pleasant, Swansea, **T** 01792 642158, www.windsor-lodge.co.uk 19 rooms. Small and friendly hotel in a welcoming grade II listed building which has the air of a country hotel yet in the city. There are elegant en suite rooms, a restaurant and convenient parking.

Guesthouses and B&Bs

B **Patrick's with Rooms**, 638 Mumbles Rd, **T** 01792 360199, www.patrickswithrooms.com Eight rooms. This restaurant-with-rooms has individually designed, contemporary bedrooms which all have a sea view. Some rooms have strong colours, others more muted shades. A couple of the bathrooms have those romantic, free-standing roll-top baths.

C **Alexandra House**, 366 Mumbles Rd, Mumbles, **T** 01792 406406, www.alexandra-house.com Six rooms. This is a comfortable four-star B&B in a white painted Victorian house on the seafront. The rooms are en suite and some have sea views. There's private parking.

C Glenview Guest House, 140 Langland Rd, Mumbles, **T** 01792 367933, www.mumblesglenview.com Six rooms. B&B in a Victorian house overlooking Underhill Park. It has en suite rooms, pretty gardens and real fires in the lounge in winter.

C Tides Reach, 388 Mumbles Rd, Mumbles, **T** 01792 404877, www.tidesreachguesthouse.co.uk Six rooms. This is a high-quality, four-star B&B on the seafront. All rooms en suite and extremely clean and comfortable. The lounge has good views over the Bay and is furnished with antiques.

D Cefn Bryn Guest House, 6 Uplands Crescent, Uplands, Swansea, **T** 01792 466687, www.cefnbryn.co.uk Conveniently located in sedate suburban Uplands, yet just a mile from the station and close to the city centre, a genuinely warm welcome awaits in this smart late-Victorian setting. Non smokers only.

D The Crescent, 132 Eaton Crescent, Uplands, Swansea, **T/F** 01792 466814, www.crescentguesthouse.co.uk Six rooms. En suite bedrooms in a roomy Edwardian guesthouse that overlooks the Bay. There are superb panoramic views from the lounge. Free private parking.

The Gower (Gwyr)

Hotels

A-L Fairyhill, Reynoldstone, Gower, **T** 01792 390139, **F** 01792 391358, www.fairyhill.net *Off A4118*. Eight rooms. This is the Gower's only five-star hotel but its reputation has spread much further. An ivy-covered, 18th-century house tucked away in the quiet of the countryside, it's a great place to luxuriate and treat yourself – if you can afford it.

C-B Oxwich Bay Hotel, Oxwich Bay, Gower, **T** 01792 390329, www.oxwichbayhotel.co.uk *Off A4118*. 13 rooms. Large, traditional hotel with great situation overlooking Oxwich Bay. Try and get a room with a sea view.

C King Arthur Hotel, Higher Green, Reynoldston, Gower, **T** 01792 390775, www.kingarthurhotel.co.uk *Off A4118*. Lovely recently refurbished rooms at this warm and popular inn, situated on the village green. Ask for a room in the pretty new annexe and you don't have to worry about noise from the bar. Recommended.

Guesthouses and B&Bs

C Surf Sound Guest House, Long Acre, Oxwich, Gower, **T** 01792 390822, www.surfsound.co.uk *Off A4118*. Five rooms. Good-value non-smoking B&B with en suite rooms, convenient for Oxwich beach. Closed in winter

C Woodside Guest House, Oxwich, Gower, **T** 01792 390791, www.oxwich.fsnet.co.uk Five rooms. This is a 200-year-old cottage that's been converted into a four-star guesthouse very conveniently situated for Oxwich beach – a good bet for surfers who can't wait to get into the water.

D-C Parc-le-Breos, Parkmill, Gower, **T** 01792 371636, www.par-le-breos.co.uk *Off A4118*. 10 rooms. 19th-century hunting lodge set in its own grounds. The rooms are clean, with en suite facilities, and many have pleasant views of the gardens. Popular with those on riding, surfing or walking holidays. Evening meals available.

D GlanGwendraeth Farm, Priory St, Kidwelly, **T** 01554 890309, www.glangwendraeth.co.uk *Off A4118 west of Llanelli*. This is a very clean and comfortable farmhouse B&B, all rooms en suite, some with views of Kidwelly's stunning (and often forgotten) castle. Good value.

D Tallizmand, Llandmadoc, Gower, **T** 01792 386373. *Off B4295.* Small, comfortable B&B, with two en suite rooms and one with shared bathroom. In the quiet village of Llandmadoc and convenient for nearby beaches and walks. Evening meals and packed lunches available.

Carmarthen (Caerfyddin) and around

Hotels

A-L Hurst House, East Marsh, Laugharne, **T** 01994 427417, **F** 01994 427730 www.hurst-house.co.uk *Off A4066 near Laugharne.* Four rooms. Actor Neil Morrissey (who also has a share in the local **New Three Mariners** pub) part owns this country-house hotel, which goes in for contemporary luxury and is aimed at the wealthy weekender market. There's also a restaurant – if you're not staying, you'll have to book in advance.

C Allt y Golau Uchaf, Felingwm Uchaf, near Carmarthen, **T** 01267 290455, www.visit-carmarthenshire.co.uk/alltygolau *On B4310, north of A40 between Carmarthan and Llandeilo.* Three rooms. Very comfortable and clean accommodation in a restored farmhouse in a peaceful location – it's on the side of the B4310. There's no TV in the rooms, but they have an immaculate residents lounge and great home baking.

Monmouthshire

Hotels

A-L Celtic Manor Resort, Coldra Woods, Newport, **T** 01633 410262, www.celtic-manor.com *Off Jct 24 of M4.* If you're keen to stay near the centre of Newport then this five-star hotel offers the swankiest, 'plus-fours-must-be-worn', type facilities. It's an outwardly ugly and unmissable building, but makes up for it with masses of leisure facilites and an adjoining golf course. It's been chosen as the venue for the Ryder cup in 2010 – so golfing heaven then.

B-A Glen-Yr-Afon-House, Pontypool Rd, Usk, **T** 01291 672302, www.glen-yr-afon.co.uk *By A472 near Usk town centre.* 28 rooms. Secluded country house in its own grounds, just a few minutes' walk from the centre of Usk. They serve home-cooked food and have a bar.

D Castle View Hotel, 16 Bridge Street, Chepstow, **T** 01291 620349, www.hotelschepstow.co.uk *Chepstow town centre.* Traditional hotel in the centre of town with a pleasant 'pubby' feel dating back 300 years. Comfortable and very convenient for the castle, as the name suggests.

Guesthouses and B&Bs

B The Bell at Skenfrith, Skenfrith, Monmouthshire, **T** 01600 750235, www.thebellatskenfrith.co.uk *Off B4521.* Eight rooms. On the banks of the River Monnow, this romantic former coaching inn has been restored to its 17th-century glory. Its smart bedrooms come complete with widescreen TVs and DVDs. Closed Mon from Nov-Mar.

C-B The Inn at the Elm Tree, St Brides, Wentlooge, near Newport, **T** 01633 680225, www.the-elm-tree.co.uk *Off B4239 near Newport.* Tucked away among flatlands and reed beds, in an area that looks more like Holland than Wales, is this refreshingly comfortable five-star inn. The rooms are individually designed, and there are books, pot plants and magazines dotted around. It's a good base for walking, watching wildlife or golfing – and also makes a great romantic hideaway.

D First Hurdle, 9 Upper Church Street, **T** 01291 622189. *Central Chepstow.* Central, down-to-earth B&B that's in a handy location for all the sights.

D Pendragon, 18 Cross Street, Caerleon, **T** 01633 430871. *Central Chepstow.* Friendly and accommodating B&B. Rooms are clean and comfy, and you eat breakfast at a large wooden table – there's homemade bread, lots of fresh fruit if you want and veggies catered for. Packed lunches if you ask.

Caerphilly and the Valleys

Hotels

B Heritage Park Hotel, Coed Cae Rd, Trehafod, near Pontypridd, **T** 01443 687057, **F** 01443 687060, www.heritageparkhotel.co.uk *Next to the Rhondda Heritage Park Museum on the A470, Pontypridd* 44 en suite rooms, parking. Comfortable and clean business-geared hotel that makes a good base for exploring the valleys and is right next to the Rhondda Heritage Park. Character is added with old photographs of mining families and landscapes hanging from the walls. They've got friendly staff and good leisure facilities, including a swimming pool, sauna, gym and beauty treatments.

Guesthouses and B&Bs

C Cottage Guest House, Pwll-y-pant, Caerphilly, **T** 02920 869160, www.smoothhound.co.uk/hotels/cottagegh.html *1 mile from Caerphilly near Jct of A468 and A469.* Three rooms, all en suite, This 300-year-old cottage has all stone walls, original beams and inglenook fireplaces. Friendly welcome and hearty breakfasts.

C Mill Farm, Cwmafon, Pontypool, **T** 01495 774588. *Off A4043, 2 miles north of Pontypool.* Three rooms. This 15th-century farmhouse B&B in the Valleys has en suite rooms, log fires and a small indoor heated swimming pool. It's adults only, as the idea is to give you complete peace and quiet.

D Tyn-y-Wern Country House, Ynysybwl, Rhonnda Cynon Taff, near Pontypridd, **T** 01443 790551. *3 miles from Pontypridd on B4273.* This is a former Victorian mine manager's house with three rooms, one en suite. They are happy to cater for walkers and cyclists. They also have self-catering lodges sleeping two to four people.

Brecon Beacons National Park

Hotels

A Allt-yr-Ynys Country House Hotel, Walterstone, near Abergavenny, **T** 01873 890307, www.allthotel.co.uk *5 miles north of Abergavenny, off A465.* Technically this comfortable and reliable hotel is in England – by about a foot: the border, the River Monnow flows beside it. It's in a secluded location, with many rooms in converted outbuildings dotted around the grounds, giving you extra privacy. There's also a swimming pool and a restaurant.

A-B The Bear Hotel, Crickhowell, **T** 01873 810408, www.bearhotel.co.uk *Crickhowell town centre*. Lovely old coaching inn dating back to 1432, the Bear has individually decorated rooms – some with wonderfully relaxing jacuzzi baths or four-poster beds. The hotel bar has plenty of character, with traditional oak beams, a flagstone floor and lots of nooks and crannies. Recommended.

B The Angel Hotel, 15 Cross St, Abergavenny, **T** 01873 857121, **F** 858059, www.angelhotelabergavenny.co.uk *Abergavenny town centre*. 29 rooms. Famous old coaching inn in the centre of Abergavenny offering plush, recently refurbished rooms, one with a four-poster bed. They also do afternoon teas.

C The Manor Hotel, Brecon Road, Crickhowell, **T** 01873 810212, www.manorhotel.co.uk *On A40 northwest of Crickhowell*. Swish hotel perched on a hill outside Crickhowell, which also has leisure facilities. Dark wooden floors and heraldry shields on the walls downstairs, while bedrooms are lighter and brighter.

C Ty Croeso Hotel, Dardy, near Crickhowell, **T** 01873 810573, www.wiz.to/tycroeso *Off B4558, ½ mile outside Crickhowell*. Eight rooms. This small hotel overlooks the Usk Valley and is close to the Brecon and Monmouthshire Canal. There's a good-quality restaurant and a welcoming atmosphere.

Guesthouses and B&Bs

B Felin Fach Griffin, near Brecon, **T** 01874 620111, www.eatdrinksleep.ltd.uk *3 miles north of Brecon on the A470*. It's hard to miss this lovely rosy-pink, refurbished pub. It's a very modern inn, which has seven individually designed, simple and stylish bedrooms. It's all contemporary and unfussy but very comfortable. As they say outside, it's a place to 'Eat, Drink, Sleep'. Got that?

C **Beacons Guest House**, 16 Bridge St, Brecon, **T** 01874 623339, www.beacons.brecon.co.uk *Central Brecon*. 14 rooms, 11 en suite. Traditional guest house in a restored Georgian townhouse. It's non smoking, and is situated just over the Usk Bridge, a few minutes from the centre of town. They also do evening meals most nights from 1830-2100.

C **Blaencar Farm**, Sennybridge, near Brecon, **T** 01874 636610, www.blaencar.co.uk *8 miles west of Brecon, off A4067*. Three rooms. This is a working farm offering good-quality B&B in a refurbished farmhouse. One room's got a four-poster bed. It's a lovely relaxing place from which to explore the National Park.

C **Felin Glais**, Aberyscir, near Brecon, **T/F** 01874 623107, www.felinglais.zookitec.com *3 miles from Brecon*. Three rooms. This is a carefully restored 17th-century barn on the outskirts of Brecon, and worth seeking out. Two of their rooms have jacuzzi baths and they serve evening meals using fresh, seasonal produce. They'll cater for veggies and vegans.

C **Ffordd-Fawr**, Glasbury, near Hay-on-Wye, **T** 01497 847332, www.ffordd-fawr.co.uk *Off B4350, 3 miles south west of Hay*. Restored farmhouse offering non-smoking accommodation in countryside close to Hay.

C **Pickwick House**, St Johns Rd, Brecon, **T** 01874 624322, www.pickwick-house.brecon.co.uk *Central Brecon*. Three en suite rooms. Non-smoking B&B in estate just minutes from the centre of town. Has a small conservatory residents can use and drying facilities for walkers and cyclists. They're happy to cater for special diets.

C **Tinto House**, Broad St, Hay-on-Wye, **T** 01497 820590, www.tintohouse.co.uk *Central Brecon*. This central B&B is in a listed Georgian townhouse, with a garden that overlooks the River Wye.

C-D **The Old Post Office**, Llanigon, near Hay-on-Wye, **T** 01497 820008, www.oldpost-office.co.uk *Off B4350 near Hay.* Three rooms. High-quality, vegetarian B&B a couple of miles from Hay. The house is a 17th-century listed building with plenty of character, and is close to Offa's Dyke Path. They also own **Oxford Cottage**, Oxford Rd, Hay-on-Wye (same **T** number, www.oxford cottage.co.uk) which has three rooms. Here they'll provide you with all the ingredients for breakfast and you make it yourself.

D **Gwyn Deri**, Mill St, Crickhowell, **T/F** 01873 810297, smith@gwynderi.fsnet.co.uk *Central Crickhowell.* Three rooms, two en suite. Clean, comfortable B&B just on the edge of town.

Hostels

F **Bunkhouse**, The Held, Cantref, near Brecon, **T** 01874 624646, www.theheldbunkhouse.co.uk *About 3 miles south of Brecon off A40.* 24-30 beds. Converted barn offering bunkhouse accommodation across six rooms. Open year round.

F **Cantref Bunkhouse**, Upper Cantref Farm, Cantref, near Brecon, **T** 01874 665223, www.cantref.com *3½ miles from Brecon.* 24 beds This three-star farm bunkhouse about three miles from Brecon accommodates 2-8 per shared room, and grounds where you can pitch a tent. Open all year. Kitchens and showers.

F **YHA Hostel**, Capel y Ffin, **T** 01873 890650. *1 mile north of Capel y Ffin.* Former hill farm now offering hostel accommodation in remote, and extremely beautiful, area.

Eating and drinking

If you thought Welsh food meant stodgy meat and potatoes washed down with beer, then eating out in Cardiff is going to be a pleasant surprise. The capital has erupted with restaurants and brasseries and you can dine on French, Turkish or Thai food, if you wish. High-quality Welsh produce is well represented and you should look for Welsh mountain beef, Salt Marsh lamb, and all sorts of seafood. There are loads of great cheeses too. Chefs often take classic dishes and give them a Welsh twist, and the contemporary trend for mixing foods and flavours has found a place on many menus. Cardiff's many café/bars allow you to pick up a light meal or snack during the day – and many places do cheap lunchtime specials. Al-fresco dining is popular, and on fine days you can hardly move for shiny metal tables and chairs spilling on to the streets. At night the atmosphere changes, with drinking taking precedence, especially at weekends, though there are still many cheap takeaway outlets catering for the post-pub crowd.

Eating codes

Price

£££	£20 and over
££	£10-20
£	£10 and under

Prices refer to the cost of a two-course meal excluding drinks or service charge.

So what are you likely to eat in Wales? Traditional breakfasts in Wales to be expected include the full fry-up (fried egg, bacon, sausages, tomatoes, mushrooms, baked beans and black pudding), scrambled egg and boiled egg with toast soldiers. The more sophisticated palate will be pleased to find Cardiff offers all manner of alternatives, including high quality restaurants with gourmet food at a reasonable price.

Pubs are still a major social hub, and pub food has been transformed in recent years. Many so-called 'gastro-pubs' serve ambitious lunchtime and suppertime menus. Keep your eye out too for tea rooms. The cream tea reaches its apotheosis in Wales, where the quality of the fresh clotted cream served up with warm scones and jam can be exceptional, and is perfect for a mid-afternoon snack, especially if you have a sweet tooth.

For a cheap meal, your best bet is a pub, hotel or café, where you can have a one-course meal for around £6-7 or less, though don't expect gourmet food. The best value is often at lunchtime, when many restaurants offer three-course set lunches or business lunches for less that £10. Also good value are the pre-theatre menus in restaurants, and you don't need a theatre ticket to take them up on the offer.

The biggest problem with eating out is the limited serving hours in most pubs and hotels. They may only serve food between 1230 and 1400, and 1700 and 1900. In smaller towns, finding food outside these hours can be a challenge.

City Centre

Restaurants

£££-££ Da Venditto, 7-8 Park Place, **T** 02920 230781. *Tue-Sat 1200-1430, 1800-2245.* *Map 2, E9, p238* Award-winning Italian restaurant offering sophisticated cuisine close to the theatre. Mains might include Gressingham duck with pea and broad bean risotto, or ravioli with spinach, baby courgettes and parmesan. Special lunchtime set menus make for a more affordable option.

££ Ask, 24/32 Wyndham Arcade, Mill Lane, **T** 02920 344665. *Mon-Sat 1200-2300, Sun 1200-2230.* *Map 2, H7, p238* Blue tablecloths and candles at this small, but sleek, contemporary Italian restaurant that attracts lots of couples. The menu includes all the usual Italian favourites and there's a long list of pizzas to choose from topped with everything from goats' cheese to white anchovies. There are plenty of veggie dishes on offer.

££ Juboraj, 10 Mill Lane, **T** 02920 377668. *Mon-Sat 1200-1400 (not Fri) and 1800-2400, closed all day Sun.* *Map 2, H7, p238* This highly rated South East Asian restaurant in the Café Quarter is one of a chain – there are others in Newport and other parts of Cardiff. This one has a bustling city vibe. If you want to eat cheaply then come at lunchtime when they do a good-value special deal.

££ La Fosse, 9-11 The Hayes, **T** 02920 237755. *Mon-Sat 1200-1430, 1800-0030, closed Sun.* *Map 2, G7, p238* This contemporary seafood restaurant/oyster bar is awash with palms, blue glass and chrome. It's housed downstairs in the former fish market. As well as starters like fish soup, and seafood mains like seabass and monkfish, there are plenty of meaty mains and a few veggie choices. Plus, of course, those oysters.

★ **Best**

Cool places for coffee

- Blas ar Cymru, p122
- Graze at Aveda, p123
- Cantina, p123
- Anywhere with a view at Mermaid Quay, p125
- Verdi's Knab Rock in Mumbles, p131

££ **Las Iguanas**, 8a Mill Lane, T 02920 226373, www.iguanas.co.uk *Food daily 1200-2330. Map 2, H7, p238* This is a popular Latin American bar/restaurant in the Café Quarter, with a large outdoor seating area that teems with people in summer. They do a wide selection of Mexican favourites like *enchiladas* and *fajitas*, as well as more unusual dishes like *moqueca*, a Brazilian stew with coconut and vegetables. Many are just here for the knock-out cocktails laced with tequila or Brazilian sugar cane rum. Shaken or stirred?

££ **Metropolis**, 60 Charles Street, T 02920 344300. *Daily 1200-1500, 1800-2300. Map 2, G9, p238* Sleek wooden floors, beige seats and cool customers, and a surprisingly reasonably priced menu. Mains might include pork and leek sausages with colcannon (£6.50), or stuffed aubergine and feta (£7.25). They also have a good range of puds too.

££ **Topo Gigio**, Church Street, T 02920 344794. *Mon-Fri 1200-1500, 1730-2300, Sat 1200-2330, Sun 1200-2300. Map 2, F6, p238* Enduringly popular Italian that squeezes them in night after night. It offers a wide range of tasty pastas and pizzas – some with a Welsh twist, such as pizza with tradtional Welsh laverbread, or leek and goats' cheese, or penne pasta with Welsh lamb. Recommended.

Eating and drinking

£ Blas ar Cymru, Old Library, The Hayes. *Tue-Sat 1000-1600.*
Map 2, F7, p238 Lovely contemporary café, all blond wood and
chrome, showcasing the best Welsh produce. Closed for
refurbishment at the time this book goes to press, its name will
possibly change to **Haze** when it reopens. Come in for
cappuccino, organic soup, Welsh rarebit or one of the daily
specials. They also have little tasting bowls filled with chunks of
Welsh cheeses. Recommended.

£ Cantina, 48 Charles St, **T** 02920 382882. *Tue-Fri 1100-1530, plus
Thu, Fri 1830-2230, Sat 1100-2230. Map 2, G9, p238* Lovely
Mediterranean-style café/bistro, with trendy yellow and lilac seats
and a little garden for warm days. Good-value pasta, pizza and
lunchtime ciabatta.

Cafés

Angel Hotel, Castle St, **T** 02920 64 9200. *Food served 1100-2300.
Map 2, E5, p238* Come for a cream tea of scones, cream and jam
plus tea, coffee or a herbal brew for around £4.75. They also do
Welsh cakes, sandwiches – no crusts cut off – and paninis.

Bar Essential, Windsor Place, **T** 02920 383762. *Food from
1200. Map 2, E10, p238* One of Cardiff's many busy café/bars. This
one serves sandwiches, pasta dishes and things like steak and
chips. At night it's the choice of the city's young professionals and
visiting business people.

BSB 'The Place', 11 Windsor Place, **T** 02920 238228. *Food daily
1100-1700, until 1900 Thu, Fri. Map 2, E10, p238* Café/bar
attracting a young post-work and shopping crowd. Take your
pick from a variety of sandwiches, salads, paninis, and main
courses like salmon and herb fishcakes. Service can unfortunately
be a little variable.

Cantina, 48 Charles St, **T** 02920 382883. *Mon-Fri 1030-1630, Thu-Sat 1900-2230. Map 2, G9, p238* Cool café with a sunny garden where you can sip a mid-shopping latte.

Graze at Aveda, 7 St Mary St, **T** 02920 233005. *Mon-Sat 0900-1800. Map 2, G6, p238* Small but very sleek organic/health café in the new Aveda emporium – toy with juices, imaginative salads, organic soup or a delicious piece of lavender cake. Dress is slim black trousers rather than hand-knitted jumpers.

Henry's, Park Chambers, **T** 02920 224672. *Food Mon-Thu 0900-2100, Fri, Sat 0900-1930, Sun 1200-1800. Map 2, E9, p238* Busy 80s-style chain café/bar popular with shoppers and the post-work crowd – who come for the cocktails. Sharing plates for £7.95, or more filling mains like chicken. Extra busy during happy hour.

Is it?, 12 Wharton St, **T** 02920 413600. *Food daily 1000-2100, open until 0030 Sun-Wed, 0100 Thu, Fri, 0200 Sat. Map 2, G6, p238* Large, self consciously, trendy café/bar with an enormous mirror behind the bar and a seating area upstairs as well as down. Popular with shoppers during the day, much noisier at night. Sandwiches, including BLTs from £2.95, salads, pasta dishes and mains like burgers or mussels.

St John the Baptist Church, near Church St. *Mon, Wed, Fri and alternate Thu lunchtimes. Map 2, F7, p238* If you need to fill up on a budget, pop in here: the WI serve soup, rolls and homemade cakes in the church – and, no, they're not naked.

Toad at the Exhibition, 18-19 Trinity St, **T** 02920 666566. *Food daily 1100-1900, bar until late. Map 2, F7, p238* The Old Library is now partly given over to this chain bar, which has a few seats outside and is convenient if you're shopping. Choose from sandwiches, paninis or wraps.

Delis and takeaways

Atlantic Coffee Company, High St Arcade/St Mary St, **T** 02920 232202. *Mon-Sat early-1800, Sun 1000-1700. Map 2, F6, p238* Coffee shop serving lattes, frothy capps, and large sandwiches and cakes to go.

Central Market, High St. *Mon-Sat 0800-1730. Map 2, F6, p238* Stalls selling fruit, veg, fabulous cheeses, bread and enormous slices of cake.

Cornish Bakehouse, 11 Church St, **T** 02920 665041. *Mon-Sat 0900-1800, Sun 1100-1700. Map 2, F6, p238* Enormous Cornish pasties to take away, with everything from the traditional filling to ones with lamb and mint, beef curry, and cheese and mushroom. Also thick-cut sandwiches.

Wally's Deli, 42 Royal Arcade, **T** 02920 229265. *Mon-Sat 0800-1730. Map 2, G6, p238* Good deli stocking Welsh cheeses, lots of Greek delicacies, Turkish Delight and other goodies.

Cathays

£££ The Armless Dragon, 97-99 Wyeverne Rd, Cathays, **T** 02920 382357. *Tue-Fri 1200-1400, Mon-Wed 1900-2100, Fri, Sat 1900-2130, booking advised. Map 1, C9, p236* Dull exterior hides an award-winning restaurant offering a new twist on Welsh dishes. Lots of lamb, chicken and fish – as well as choices for veggies like, ahem , laverballs. There's a good choice of Welsh wines and cheeses – and cinnamon bread and butter pudding.

££ The Greenhouse, 38 Woodville Rd, Cathays, **T** 02920 235731. *Tue-Sun 1100-1500, plus Tue-Sat from 1900. Map 1, C9, p236*

A good vegetarian and seafood restaurant out in Cathays, offering imaginative dishes. Influences are international, while the produce is fresh and local – often organic. Look out for things like roquefort tart with red onion jam, or leek, black olive and goats' cheese in filo pastry. Puddings might include an almond and quince tart.

Delis and takeways

Forum Deliciae, corner of Richards St and Crwys Rd, Cathays, **T/F** 02920 373077. *Mon-Sat 0900-1800. Map 1, C9, p236* Fab European deli run by friendly George Exintaris, who also imports food and wine from Europe.

Cardiff Bay

Restaurants

£££ Tides, St David's Hotel and Spa, Havana St, **T** 02920 313018. *Mon-Thu 1200-1430, 1800-2200; Fri, Sat 1230-1430, 1800-2230, Sun 1230-1500, 1800-2200. Map 3, H1, p240* Marco Pierre White created the menus for this sophisticated restaurant in the five-star hotel. You get also get some lovely views over Cardiff Bay, crisp white cloths and fresh flowers on the table. Definitely the place to bring folk you want to impress.

£££ Woods Brasserie, Pilotage Building, Stuart St, **T** 02920 492400. *Daily 1200-1430, 1900-2200, booking recommended. Map 3, G1, p240* Upmarket modern brasserie in a listed building in the Bay, now light and modern inside with lots of glass and an open–plan kitchen. They serve excellent food that has distinct Asian influences – perhaps oriental crispy beef salad or sweet and sour salmon. Traditional fish and chips with beer batter is also very popular.

£££-££ Scallops, Mermaid Quay, **T** 02920 497495. *Mon-Thu 1200-1430, 1900-2130; Fri 1200-1430, 1900-2230; Sat 1200-1500, 1900-2230, Sun 1200-1600.* Map 3, G2, p240 This light, airy restaurant with views of the waterfront serves sophisticated seafood, as well as a few meaty dishes.

££ Bosphorus, Mermaid Quay, **T** 02920 487477. *Mon-Fri 1200-1500, 1800-midnight; Sat, Sun 1400-1700, 1800-2400.* Map 3, G2, p240 Perched on a jetty, this glass-sided Turkish restaurant has great views around the Bay. The food's a reminder that Turkish cuisine doesn't have to be a dodgy doner kebab after the pub.

££ Izakaya, Mermaid Quay, **T** 02920 492939. *Mon-Sat 1200-1430, 1800-2300, Sun 1300-2200.* Map 3, G2, p240 If you fancy something light like tempura, then make for this Japanese restaurant. You can dine Japanese-style on low tables if you choose, and staff are kitted out in kimonos. As you'd expect, there's lots of fish (including a dish featuring raw tuna) and you can wash it all down with sake or Japanese beer. Hai!

££ Signor Valentino, Mermaid Quay, **T** 02920 482007. *Daily 1100-2300.* Map 3, G2, p240 This airy eaterie pleases the punters by offering all the usual Italian eats coupled with some great views over Cardiff Bay.

££-£ Bar Cwtsh, 5 Bute Crescent, **T** 07815 125130. *Opening hours tbc.* Map 3, F3, p240 Due to open in late summer 2004 this restaurant and wine bar at Jolyon's Hotel plans to serve quality food like homemade soups, sandwiches, and bangers and mash.

££-£ Salt, Mermaid Quay, Stuart St, Cardiff Bay, **T** 02920 494375. *Mon-Thu 1000-2300, Fri-Sat 1000-0100, Sun 1000-2230.* Map 3, G2, p240 This slick bar/restaurant offers a range of pasta dishes and sharing plates in the heart of the revitalised Bay.

££-£ Terra Nova, Mermaid Quay, Stuart St, **T** 02920 450947. *Mon-Sat 1100-2300, Fri-Sat 1100-0100, Sun noon-2230. Map 3, G2, p240* The food in this bar/restaurant ranges from simple bar snacks to full meals, and the choice is excellent.

City suburbs

Restaurants

£££ Le Gallois - Y Cymro, 6-10 Romilly Crescent, Canton, **T** 02920 341264, www.legallois-ycymro.com *Tue-Sat 1200-1430, 1830-2230, booking advised. Map 1, D7, p236* This family-run bistro offers award-winning French-influenced food for discerning, well-heeled diners. One of Cardiff's top places to eat, it serves dishes like langoustine risotto. Very posh, very French.

£££ The Old Post Office, Greenwood Lane, St Fagans, **T** 02920 565400. *Thu-Sun 1200-1400, Wed-Sat 1900-2130. Map 1, C1, p236* A few miles outside the city centre, this restaurant serves high-quality, come-for-a-treat, modern European food. You might find goat's cheese soufflée, fillet of Welsh beef or duck ravioli on the menu. Leave room for a pudding though – the French pastry chef produces calorie-filled treats such as pistachio crème brûlée, and brioches filled with prunes and armagnac.

££ Happy Gathering, 233 Cowbridge Rd East, **T** 02920 397531. *Mon-Thu 1200-2300, Fri, Sat 1200-2330, Sun 1200-2230. Map 1, D6, p236* This large, busy restaurant is an enduring favourite serving an extensive range of Chinese food. It attracts a loyal following.

££ Stefanos, 14 Romilly Crescent, **T** 02920 372768. *Tue 1200-1400, Mon-Sat 1200-1400, 1900-2300. Map 1, D7, p236* This is a popular, family-run Italian restaurant out in the Canton region of the city.

Eating and drinking

££ **The Cinnamon Tree**, 173 Kings Rd, Pontcanna, **T** 02920 374433. *Mon-Thu and Sat 1200-1400, Mon-Sat 1800-2300. Map 1, D7, p236* Shiny polished wood and not a hint of flock wallpaper at this very popular Indian restaurant. All the usual curries are on the menu but you'll also find more unusual dishes like 'flaming ostrich' (it's grilled, not burn your mouth spicy), spicy duck and Bangladeshi fish. Veggies aren't neglected and can look forward to the unpronounceable *kathri kai kara kozumba* (baby aubergine in a yoghurty sauce). Booking's essential at weekends.

£ **Cibo**, 83 Pontcanna St, **T** 02920 232226. *Mon 1200-2100, Tue-Sun 1000-2200, booking advisable. Map 1, C7, p236* Great Italian place, good for daytime or evenings. Good value ciabatta, pizzas and pastas in friendly atmosphere.

Vale of Glamorgan

Restaurants

£££-££ **Huddarts**, 69 High St, Cowbridge, **T** 01446 774645. *Tue-Sun 1200-1400, Tue-Sat 1900-2130.* Come here to taste good Welsh meats or fish – cockles and laverbread are also on the menu.

££ **Valentino's**, 44 High St, Cowbridge, **T** 01446 771155. *Thu-Sat 1215-1445, 1730-2200.* Italian restaurant serving the usual pizzas, pastas and meaty mains. Lunch and early-bird menus for £4.95.

££ **Tomlins**, 46 Plassey St, Penarth, **T** 02920 706644. *Tue-Sat from 1900 plus Fri, Sat 1200-1430, open alternate Sun 1200-1430.* Don't come expecting knit-your-own-tofu burgers. This is a high-quality veggie restaurant serving imaginative dishes such as pea cannelloni with blue cheese sauce.

££-£ **Bar 44**, 44c High St, Cowbridge, **T** 01446 776630. *Mon 1200-2100, Tue-Sat 1200-2300, Sun 1200-2230.* Lively tapas bar on the main street.

££-£ **Bokhara Brasserie**, Court Colman Manor, Pen-y-Fai, Bridgend, **T** 01656 721122. *Tue-Fri 1230-1430, 1900-2300, Sat 1900-2300, Sun 1200-1430.* Great Indian cuisine in the very unlikely setting of a rambling former manor house that has now become a hotel. It offers very good value meals, especially for vegetarians. The kitchen at one end of the restaurant is open so you can see your food being prepared, if you want to keep tabs on the chef.

££-£ **Farthings**, 54 High St, Cowbridge, **T** 01446 772990. *Mon-Fri 1000-1530, Sat 1000-1600, Sun 1000-1530, and Tue-Sat 1900-2200.* Good-value food at this bistro where you can fill up with baked potatoes, pasta or delicious salads during the day, and more substantial dishes at night.

Cafés

Gallery Espresso, 68 Eastgate, Cowbridge **T** 01446 775093. *Mon-Sat 1000-1700.* Great little café serving wide range of fresh filled baguettes, bagels and other snacks, as well as yummy homemade cakes and teas and coffees.

Delis and takeways

Glanmor's, Unit 30, Castle Court, Brynau Rd, Bridgend **T** 02920 888355. *Mon-Sat 0830-1730.* A great sandwich shop, close to the castle, serving homemade pastries and meals.

Swansea (Abertawe) and around

Restaurants

£££ Morgans, Somerset Place, Swansea, **T** 01792 484848. *Mon-Fri, Sun 1200-1500, Tue-Sat 1900-2100.* This is Swansea's special occasion venue. There are two restaurants in this upmarket hotel that's situated in the former Victorian Port Authority building. It's all non smoking, the food's highly rated and there's a champagne bar too.

£££-££ Knights Restaurant, 614-616 Mumbles Rd, **T** 01792 363184. *Mon 1830-2130, Tue-Sat 1200-1400, 1830-2130, Sun 1200-1400.* Lively, contemporary restaurant with extensive fish menu – look out for sewin (sea trout) and monkfish, as well as lots of unusual meat choices like wild boar, ostrich or guinea fowl. Separate veggie menu.

£££-££ PA's Wine Bar, 95 Newton Rd, Mumbles, **T** 01792 367723. *Daily 1200-1430, Mon-Sat 1800-2130.* This little wine bar serves Welsh food in a relaxed setting and is very popular. In summer the doors open and you can look out on to the garden. They do lots of fish, bought from the market – you might find Penclawdd mussels with white wine and garlic on the menu.

£££-££ Patrick's with Rooms, 638 Mumbles Rd, **T** 01792 360199. *Daily 1200-1420 and 1830-2150, Sun 1200-1400 only.* Imaginative British cuisine in very popular restaurant with rooms. There's a daily specials board and they use lots of Welsh produce like cockles, laverbread and Welsh beef. Dishes might include pan-fried duck with honey plum sauce, or game pie, and they also have a good choice for veggies with things like ravioli with wild mushrooms.

££ **Hanson's**, Pilot House Wharf, Trawler Rd, **T** 01792 466200. *Tue-Sun 1200-1400, Mon-Sat 1830-2130.* Catherine and Michael have been spotted in this pleasant, out of the way, restaurant. They're big on fish, which is bought fresh locally, and you might find turbot, cod, lobster or mussels. There are also a couple of options for veggies and they're happy to cater for special diets. The three-course lunch for £13.95 is good value.

££ **La Braseria**, 28 Wind St, **T** 01792 469683. *Mon-Sat 1200-1430, 1900-2330.* Situated on Wind St, the heart of Swansea's drinking and dining area, this large restaurant/wine bar serves Mediterranean dishes and a dash of Spanish music. Downstairs is mainly meat, upstairs fish. It's popular so gets very busy.

£ **Claudes**, 93 Newton Rd, Mumbles, **T** 01792 366006, www.claudes.org.uk *Mon-Fri 1200-1430,1800-2200, Sat 1200-1430, 1800-2145, Sun 1200-1500.* Inventive Welsh/British cuisine in simple restaurant. Dishes such as homemade meatballs, roast cod with red pepper sauce, pan-fried Welsh black beef with chilli jam, or saffron risotto. Two-course set lunch is a worthwhile choice on a budget.

£ **G&Ts Bistro**, 602 Mumbles Rd, **T** 01792 367309. *Mon 1830-2130, Tue-Sat 1200-1400, 1830-2130, Sun 1200-1500, 1900-2130.* Warm red interior and flickering candles at this bistro which serves mains like Welsh beef and lamb, as well as tapas.

£ **Govindas**, 8 Cradock St, Mumbles, **T** 01792 468469. *Mon-Sat 1000-1800.* Established Hare Krishna veggie diner offering good-value grub. Good karma if not sophisticated.

£ **Verdi's Knab Rock**, Mumbles Rd, **T** 01792 369135, www.verdis-café.co.uk *Daily 1000-2100 (2200 Jul and Aug), earlier closing Mon-Thu in winter.* Laid-back Italian ice cream parlour and restaurant, with great views across Swansea Bay. Great for relaxing outside with a waist-expanding ice cream sundae, pizzas, foccacia or just coffee.

Cafés

Café Valance, 50 Newton Rd, Mumbles, **T** 01792 367711. *Mon-Sat 0800-1800.* Great café with lots of comfy sofas and a good choice of filled baguettes, panini, cakes and coffees.

The Coffee Denn, 34 Newton Rd, Mumbles, **T** 01792 360044. *Mon-Sat 1000-1730, Sun 1100-1730.* Good place for snacks, light meals like jacket potatoes, and heartier options such as chicken casserole or cottage pie.

Delis and takeaways

Deli 28, Newton Rd, Mumbles, **T** 01792 366828. *Tue-Sat 0930-1730.* This is a great place to pick up cheeses, olives and other picnic items.

The Gower (Gwyr)

Restaurants

£££ Fairyhill, Reynoldstone, off B4295, **T** 01792 390139. *Daily 1230-1330, 1730-2045.* If you can't afford to spend the night at this luxurious country hotel you can still enjoy some of its comforts in the restaurant, which uses local produce and serves classical, highly rated food with a contemporary twist. Good choice of wines and delicious desserts too. Lunch is good value.

££ **Welcome to Town Inn**, Llanrhidian, on B4295 and B4271, **T** 01792 390015, www.thewelcometotown.co.uk *Tue-Sun 1200-1400, Tue-Sat 1900-2130*. Highly-acclaimed food at this award-winning bistro. They've got lots of Welsh produce on the menu and do good-value set lunches. There's a good choice of Welsh cheese, homemade bread and fresh vegetables.

££-£ **King Arthur Hotel**, Higher Green, Reynoldston, off A4118, **T** 01792 390775. *Daily 1200-1430, 1800-2100 (2130 at weekends)*. Lively inn on the village green, with a large inglenook fireplace and nautical theme in the cosy bar. Wide choice of bar meals with several veggie options.

££-£ **Oxwich Bay Hotel**, Oxwich Bay, **T** 01792 390329. *Off A4118. Food available all day*. Plenty of choice of no-nonsense food here, with dishes like baked potatoes, sausages or burgers as well as pricier food like steaks and seabass. The terrace offers a great outlook over the beach.

£ **King's Head**, Llangennith, **T** 01792 386212. *Off B4295. Food 1100-2130 Mon-Sat, Sun 1200-2130*. Popular pub serving bar meals like lamb balti, goulash or sweet and sour chicken. Good selection of real ales.

Cafés

Talents Coffee House, Pentre Rd, St Clears, **T** 01994 231826. *Just off A40 north of Laugharne. Mon-Sat 1030-1630 and Bank Holidays*. Great contemporary café serving fresh local produce like Salt Marsh lamb hot pot, or Welsh black beef casserole, as well as veggie dishes, filled baguettes, juices, local ice cream and homemade cakes. Recommended.

Three Cliffs Coffee Shop, 68 Southgate Rd, Penard, **T** 01792 233885. *Off A4118 near Southgate. Daily 1030-1800.* Cheery green and white check tablecloths, outside seating and good homebaking at this lovely little café tucked away on the south Gower coast. Serves a good selection of filled baguettes, snacks and coffees.

Carmarthen (Caerfyddin) and around

Restaurants

£££ The Four Seasons Restaurant, Nantgaredig, **T** 01267 290238. *Off A40 east of Carmarthen. Booking essential, Tue-Sat 1930-2130, closed Sun.* This restaurant with rooms offers a four-course set menu for £25. There are slate floors, checked tablecloths and the food draws locals as well as visitors again and again. Mains like rabbit with Dijon mustard, Welsh saltmarsh lamb, or spinach and Caerphilly pancakes. The puddings are good – try the chocolate and pear tart.

£££-££ Y Polyn, Nantgaredig, **T** 01276 290000. *Off A40 east of Carmarthen. Lunches 1200-1500, evenings from 1800.* Lots of Welsh produce on the menu in this pub which has both a restaurant and bar. Serves real ales too.

££ Glasfryn, Brechfa, **T** 01267 202306. *Off B4310. Evening meals by arrangement.* This B&B happily cooks for non residents if you book. You eat in the conservatory, the food is freshly cooked – mains cost around £9.50 and might be lamb in redcurrant sauce, or cheese and parsnip roulade with apricot stuffing.

££ Halfway Inn, Nantgaredig, **T** 01558 668337. *Off A40 east of Carmarthen. Tue-Sat 1130-1430, 1800-2130, Sun 1200-1345.* Pub offering standard bar lunches, as well as more filling meals like roast duck or steak and mushroom pie. There are also some vegetarian choices.

£ **The Plough**, Felingwm-uchaf, **T** 01267 290019. *On B4310. Food Mon-Fri 1800-2100, Sat 1200-1500, 1800-2100.* Great traditional pub with oak beams and a real fire in winter. Serves 'farmers' portions' of food, some veggie choices and a good selection of real ales.

Cafés

Barita, 139 Rhosmaen St, Llandeilo, **T** 01558 823444. *Off A476. Mon-Sat from 0930-approx 1700.* Excellent deli/café serving great coffee, cakes and imaginative tarts, filled rolls and baguettes. Try your chosen cheese from the counter with sticky onion marmalade. Recommended.

The Carmarthen Coast

Restaurants

£££ **Hurst House**, East Marsh, **T** 01994 427417. *Off A4066 outside Laugharne. Daily 1200-1600, 1900-2200.* The emphasis is on fresh (and pricey) Welsh produce here. You might find mains like Welsh beef or lamb or local lobster on the menu. If you can't run to a meal you can also pop in for coffee – or even try an à la carte breakfast, available from 1100.

££-£ **Owl and the Pussycat Tea rooms**, 3 Grist Sq, Laugharne, **T** 01994 427742. *Tue-Wed, Sun 1000-1700, Thu-Sat 1000-2200.* Traditional tea rooms with Welsh cakes and bara brith to take with your tea, or evening meals like crab salad or salmon.

££-£ **Portreeve Restaurant and Tavern**, Market Sq, Laugharne, **T** 01994 427476. *Daily 1215-1430, and Tue-Sat 1830-2130, and Sun 1215-1430.* Booking advised. Good bar meals, with lots of Welsh produce as well as pizzas and other dishes. Real ales.

Monmouthshire

Restaurants

£££ **The Bell at Skenfrith**, Skenfrith, **T** 01600 750235. *A465 then off B4521.* Daily 1200-1430, 1900-2130 (2100 on Sun).* The 2 AA Rosette dining room at this popular inn offers a range of modern dishes using largely seasonal and locally sourced ingredients and a fab award-winning wine list.

£££-££ **The Inn at the Elm Tree**, St Brides, Wentlooge, near Newport, **T** 01633 680225. *Off B4239.* Mon-Sat 1200-1430, 1730-2100, Sun 1200-1500.* High-quality food at this 21st-century inn. You can have a light lunch like wild boar and apple sausages, or broadbean and tomato risotto for £7.50, or splash out and eat on crisp white linen in the restaurant in the evening. Mains are strong on fish and local produce. Good vegetarian dishes too.

££ **Castle View Hotel**, 16 Bridge St, Chepstow, **T** 01291 620349. *Central Chepstow. Daily 1200-1430, 1830-2100.* Relaxed hotel serving tasty light meals during the day, like ploughman's lunches and jacket potatoes, and more substantial evening meals.

££ **The Boat Inn**, The Back, Chepstow, **T** 01291 628192. *Central Chepstow. Mon-Sat 1200-1500, 1830-2130, Sun 1200-1500.* With a lovely waterside setting, outdoor seats and old beams, this inn is the best place in town for a drink, a snack or a good bar meal.

££ **The Bush House Bistro**, 15 Bridge St, Usk, **T** 01291 672929. *Off A449. Evenings only.* Brightly coloured tablecloths and terracotta walls make this good-quality restaurant a cheery choice on a damp evening. Dishes range from Mediterranean to Welsh and might include sea bass roasted in rock salt or Cornish cod stuffed with smoked cheese.

££ **The Grape**, 24 St Mary's St, Chepstow, **T** 01291 620959. *Central Chepstow. Food 1200-2130.* This wine bar/bistro serves baguettes, sandwiches and snacks during the day – as well as wine of course. There's a restaurant upstairs.

££ **Three Salmons Hotel**, Bridge St, Usk, **T** 01291 672133. *Off A449. Daily lunchtimes and 1800-2130 (1830-2200 Sat).* Lunchtime snacks like BLTs and ploughmans' with a varied menu in the evening with veggie dishes like cannelloni with wild mushrooms and goats cheese to meaty choices such as breast of goose.

££ **Wye Knot**, The Back, Chepstow, **T** 01291 622929. *Central Chepstow. Tue-Fri 1230-1430, 1900-2200, Sat 1900-2200, Sun 1230-1430.* Winner of two AA rosettes, this restaurant down by the river is the best place to eat in Chepstow. Sunday lunch here is a local favourite, with choices such as leg of lamb or sirloin of beef. There's loads of choice and you get homemade bread and good fresh vegetables.

Cafés

Rainbow Café, Moor St, Chepstow, **T** 01291 628795. *Central Chepstow. Mon-Sat 0930-1700.* Friendly coffee shop and Christian bookshop serving good selection of coffees, hot chocolate and cakes, sandwiches and paninis.

Delis and takeaways

Beaufort Deli, Beaufort Sq, Chepstow, **T** 01291 626190. *Central Chepstow. Mon-Sat 0900-1900, Sun 1000-1700.* Good deli offering all sorts of tartlets, quiches, cheeses, pâtés, salads and imaginative sandwiches to eat in or take away. Good place to fill your pack before setting off to walk Offa's Dyke.

Caerphilly and the Valleys

Restaurants

££ Heritage Park Hotel, Coed Cae Rd, Trehafod, near Pontypridd, **T** 01443 687057. *Off A470. 1200-1400, 1900-2200 daily.* This hotel restaurant is worth checking out if you want a change from pub grub. Lots of steaks and roast meats, as well as some good veggie choices like saffron risotto.

££-£ The Cinnamon Tree, Tonteg Rd (Power Station Hill), Treforest, near Pontypridd, **T** 01443 843222. *Off A470. Wed-Sat 1200-1400, Mon-Sat 1800-2230, Sun from 1200.* If you're out and about and suddenly yearn for a curry, this is the answer. It's a drive-through Indian restaurant. It's very popular, so you'll need to phone in your order in advance – then turn up and tuck in.

Brecon Beacons National Park

Restaurants

£££ The Walnut Tree Inn, Llandewi Skirrid, Abergavenny, **T** 01873 852797, www.thewalnutreeinn.com *A465 to Hereford, then on B4521. Closed Sun, Mon.* Well-established and highly rated restaurant that has been attracting food pilgrims (with healthy credit cards) for years.The menu recently got a revamp from Gordon Ramsay – the man who put the *f* in *chef*.

£££-££ Felin Fach Griffin, near Brecon, **T** 01874 620111. *3 miles out of town on A470. Tue-Sun 1230-1430, 1900-2130.* One of a new wave of highly rated 'gastropubs' in Wales. The interior is an eclectic mix of oak beams, stone floors and laid-back leather sofas, and the food is based on fresh local produce such as saltmarsh lamb, cheeses and locally grown salad leaves. Even AA Gill liked it.

£££-££ Kilverts, The Bullring, Hay-on-Wye, **T** 01497 821042. *Central Hay. Food 1200-1400, 1900-2130.* Very popular pub that serves great bar food. Seats outside on fine days.

£££-££ Old Black Lion, Lion St, Hay-on-Wye, **T** 01497 820841. *Central Hay. Food 1200-1430, 1830-2130.* Highly rated food in this atmospheric old inn that's got open fires and a nice cosy feel. You can splash out in the restaurant or eat more cheaply in the bar. Blackboard menus change all the time.

£££-££ The White Swan, Llanfrynach, **T** 01874 665276, www.the-white-swan.com *A few miles south of Brecon. Wed-Sun 1200-1400, 1900-2130.* Another revitalised pub, serving high-quality food, tucked away in the countryside outside Brecon. Features fresh produce and has a daily 'specials' menu with many fish dishes and several veggie choices.

££ Beacons Guest House, 16 Bridge Street, Brecon, **T** 01874 623339. *Tue-Sat 1830-2100.* Guest house restaurant which also serves non residents. Mains might include halloumi cheese with tomato and black olive sauce, or pork hock in fruit compote for around £9.95.

££ **The Bear Hotel**, Crickhowell, **T** 01873 810408. *Daily 1200-1400, evenings Mon-Sat 1900-2130.* Wide choice of very good food, with several vegetarian choices. Mains in the bar cost around £7-9 and might include homemade faggots in onion gravy; restaurant mains such as fillet of salmon with asparagus around £14.50.

££ **Nantyffin Cider Mill Inn**, Brecon Rd, Crickhowell, **T** 01873 810212. *On A40. Food 1200-1400 and 1830-2100 (1900-2100 in winter), sometimes shuts on Mon or Tue.* Lovely old, pink painted inn on the A40 out of Crickhowell, serving excellent food and real ales. Mains might include baked vegetable tart (£10.50) or roast duck (£14.95), and scrummy puds such as lemon tart. Very popular so worth booking.

££ **Pear Tree**, 6 Church St, Hay-on-Wye, **T** 01497 820777. *Thu-Sat 1200-1400, Tue-Sat 1900-2100.* This restaurant's set in an old Georgian townhouse and is all deep red and dark wood inside. There's fresh Welsh produce on the menu, which is given a zesty twist with flavours from Thailand and Morocco.

££-£ **The Angel Hotel**, 15 Cross St, Abergavenny, **T** 01873 857121. *Bar meals 1200-1430 and 1830-2200, restaurant 1900-2200.* You can choose formal meals in the restaurant of this revamped hotel, which offers mains like duck breast with red cabbage, venison with liquorice sauce or red mullet. Lighter/cheaper meals are available in the bar where you can snuggle by an open fire in winter or sit out in the courtyard during the summer.

££-£ **The Puzzle Tree**, opposite museum, Brecon, **T** 01874 610005. *Mon-Wed 1100-1100, Thu 1100-midnight, Fri, Sat 1100-0100, Sun 1200-2230.* Large modern-looking place attracting a younger crowd. Does a bit of everything, serving breakfasts from 0900-1200, cream teas in the afternoon, and evening meals such as curries, steaks and veggie choices from around £6.95-13.95.

Cafés

Blue Boar, Castle St, Hay-on-Wye, **T** 01497 820884. *Coffees from 0930, light meals 1200-1800, more expensive choices in the evening.* Friendly café/bar where you can get light snacks like hummous with pitta bread, sandwiches and cakes through to more substantial mains like Tuscan bean casserole served with couscous (£7.95).

The Café, 39 High St, Brecon. *Mon-Sat 1000-1700.* Busy, popular licensed café with nice bright décor of white painted floors and shocking pink chairs. Serves fair-trade coffees, soups, cakes, and baguettes stuffed with fillings like brie and grape, beef and horseradish or goats cheese, rocket and pine nuts.

The Cheese Press, 18 High St, Crickhowell, **T** 01873 810167. *Daily 0930-1500 (1330 on Wed).* Coffee shop at the back of a gift shop serving good cakes, and light meals like toasties or curry and lentil pasties.

The Granary, Broad St, Hay-on-Wye, **T** 01497 820884. *Food daily 1000-2100.* Another very popular, relaxed self-service café, with green plastic cloths on the tables, wooden floors and good food. It is a great spot for soup, salads, sandwiches or just a coffee, cake and a read of the newspaper. Plenty of veggie and vegan main meal choices.

Oscars, High Town, Hay-on-Wye, **T** 01497 821193. *Daily 1030-1630.* Very busy, good-value self-service café, with scrubbed pine tables and wooden floors – hard to get a seat at peak times. Great place for bowls of soup, delicious cakes, or substantial main meals. Always plenty for veggies.

Delis and takeaways

Mad Hatters, Cross St, Abergavenny, **T** 01873 859839. *Daily 0930-1730.* Excellent sandwich/coffee bar where you can eat in or take away. Delicious pâtisserie, sponge cakes and sandwiches, such as brie, grape and apple, and mozzarella, tomato and avocado.

Most of the constantly changing bars, pubs and clubs are in the city centre and Cardiff Bay. Mill Lane, otherwise known as the 'Café Quarter', offers a fair choice of eating options and bars. Gay venues focus on Charles Street and elsewhere on the city's southern fringe. Wednesday night sees the university crowds descend on the town for student nights at various venues. Fridays and Saturdays can be incredibly rowdy, when assorted South Walians and stag and hen crowds (hens generally wearing antlers or sprouting sparkly fairy wings) go largin' it in the big city. But many bars, pubs and clubs are now competing for punters during the rest of the week, with cheap drinks, late licences and live band nights. These days the city seems to be crammed with themed chain pubs. However, traditional pubs still exist. The locally brewed beer is Brains – shipped, so some said, to the US for Catherine Zeta-Jones and Michael Douglas' wedding bash in order to keep her Welsh relatives happy.

City Centre

Bars

Bar Ice, 4 Churchill Way, **T** 02920 237177. *Sun-Tue, Thu and Fri 1100-2300, Wed and Sat 1100-0200.* Map 2, F9, p238 Popular with students and office workers, this chrome bar is perfect if you're vain as there are plenty of mirrors in which to admire yourself. If you can see through the smoky atmosphere and hear yourself above the laughter and general buzz, as well as the sport on TV.

City Arms, Quay St, **T** 02920 225258. *Mon-Sat 1100-2300, Sun 1100-22.30.* Map 2, E5, p238 Busy bar that almost overflows on match days. Best not to say anything rude about the Welsh rugby or football teams here.

Copa, 4 Wharton St, **T** 02920 222114. *1100-2300.* Map 2, G6, p238 Large, stylish mirrored bar in former glass factory offering a wide range (around 14 so far) of European beers from places like Belgium, Italy and Germany. They also serve food.

Cuba, Unit 9, The Friary, **T** 02920 397967. *Mon-Sat 1100-0200, closed Sun.* Map 2, E7, p238 Small bar gets cramped towards the weekend with drinkers, gawpers, pullers and people shaking their thing to salsa and merengue – take classes if your footwork isn't up to scratch, they run them on Tue.

Ha!Ha! Bar and Canteen, The Friary, **T** 02920 397997. *Mon-Thu 1100-2300, Fri 1100-2400, Sat 1000-2400, Sun 1000-2230.* Map 2, E7, p238 This bar is perfect for chilling out after a hard day's shopping, or for posing after dark – it aims to be all things to all (thirtysomething) people. A wide selection of snacks, main meals and desserts is also on offer – one of Cardiff's best new bars.

Life, St Mary St, **T** 02920 667800. *Mon-Sat 1200-0100, Sun 1200-1230. Map 2, H6, p238* Popular with young professional types who are thirsty but wouldn't be seen dead in one of Life's pub-chain neighbours. This still does not explain the long queues on Fri and Sat.

Moloka, 7 Mill Lane, **T** 02920 225592. *Mon 1700-2400, Tue-Wed 1200-0100, Thu-Sat 2400-0200, Sun 1700-2400. Map 2, H7, p238* Lively vodka bar with a small dancefloor, doing a popular line in cocktails too. Regular DJ nights.

Sugar, 23 Womanby St, **T** 02920 343433. *Mon-Sat 1700-0200, some daytimes too. Map 2, E5, p238* This is Cardiff's newest style bar, located in a converted warehouse on a cobbled street. It covers several floors and each one is slightly different in shades of chocolate, pink and magenta. Lots of cocktails and ecclectic, soulful music.

The Cottage, 25 St Mary's St, **T** 02920 337194. *Mon-Sat 1100-2300, Sun 1200-2230. Map 2, G6, p238* Popular traditional Edwardian pub in the centre of the city, serving real ales and attracting people of all ages – Dads love it. Food at lunchtimes.

The Old Arcade, 14 Church St, **T** 02920 231740. *Mon-Sat 1100-2300, Sun 1100-22.30. Map 2, F6, p238* An old-fashioned pub serving Brains beer as well as bar food. Packed on rugby international days, it is loved by locals and visitors alike.

Clubs

Clwb Ifor Bach, 11 Womanby St, **T** 02920 232199, www.clwb.net *Tue and Wed 2100-0200, Thu-Sat 2000-0200, sometimes earlier if live bands are playing. Map 2, E5, p238* Situated over three floors, it is regarded as one of the coolest clubs in Cardiff thanks to a popular mix of regular live music and DJs. Saturday is for members only (be they Welsh speaking or Welsh learners).

Flares, 96 St Mary St, **T** 02920 235825. *Open till 0100. Map 2, G6, p238* This is a real blast from the past. An eclectic clientele from Rocky Horror wannabees to alcopopped teens – if you're up for dressing up in glittery Afros and grooving to Seventies hits, this one's for you.

Metros, Bakers Row, **T** 02920 399939. *Tue-Sat. Entry £5.* Rockers heaven, this club bangs out sweaty rock and metal music – at its loudest on Tuesday which is student night.

No 10, 10 Mill Lane, **T** 02920 645000. *Mon, Thu, Sat 2100-0100. Map 2, H7, p238* This classy club is in fact three clubs in one, full of designer-clad crowds of chic folk who happen to pass the No 10 doorstep test.

Stylus, Elgin House, Golate, **T** 02920 376110. *Map 2, G6, p238* There are three bars at this small venue which majors on house music. There's quite a strict dress code so don't turn up in scruffy old trainers.

The Emporium, 8-10 High St, **T** 02920 66 4577. *Tue, Fri and Sat. Map 2, E6, p238* Dance club that hosts a variety of club nights with visiting big-name DJs, spread over 2 floors. Something for everyone, especially the diehard clubmonster.

The Sodabar, 41 St Mary St, **T** 02920 238181, www.thesodabar.com *Thu-Sat 2200-late . Map 2, G6, p238* Pitching for the more discerning end of the clubbing market, its chic interior is packed to the gunnels with Italian furniture on flagstone floors. Great DJs and an excellent sound system add to the buzzy atmosphere.

Toucan Club, 5-97 St Mary's St, **T** 02920 372212, www.toucanclub.co.uk *Tue-Sun. Map 2, G6, p238* A unique and independent venue in Cardiff, this chilled yet friendly club hosts live music with an eclectic global flavour upstairs, and often features salsa and Latin American music.

Cardiff Bay

Bars

City Canteen, 1-2 Mount Stuart Square, **T** 02920 331020. *Mon-Fri 1000-2300, Sat 1200-2300, Sun 1200-2230. Map 3, F2, p240* Cool bar in the Bay – unlikely to attract squealing crowds of celebrating hens.

Salt, Mermaid Quay, Stuart St, **T** 02920 494375. *Mon-Thu 1000-2300, Fri-Sat 1000-0100, Sun 1000-2230. Map 3, G2, p240* New England-style bar, complete with arty driftwood over two floors and stylish comfortable sofas.

Terra Nova, Mermaid Quay, Stuart St, **T** 02920 450947. *Mon-Sat 1100-2300, Fri-Sat 1100-0100, Sun 1200-2230. Map 3, G2, p240* Set on four levels, the building is shaped like a ship's bow. A seating area on the top floor resembling a crow's nest is ideal for people-watching on a summer's evening.

The Waterguard, Harbour Drive, **T** 02920 499034. *Mon-Sat 1100-2300, Sun 1100-2230. Map 3, H3, p240* The main bar area is modern and open, with comfy sofas in light and airy surroundings.

Bars and clubs

Taff dancing

Cardiff's club scene is as eclectic and energetic as the country's renowned musical heritage.

Clubs

Evolution, UCI building, Atlantic Wharf, **T** 02920 464444. *Wed, Fri 2200-0200, Sat 2130-0400. Map 3, E4, p240* The biggest club in Cardiff, it offers cheap booze, party anthems and mainstream house and dance. There is a free bus service to collect would-be groovers from outside the New Theatre in the city, every 15 minutes from 2115. You may well wonder why...

City suburbs

Bars

Cayo Arms, 36 Cathedral Rd, Pontcanna, **T** 02920 391910. *Mon-Sat 1100-2300, Sun 1100-2230. Map 1, D8, p236* Named after a commander of the Free Wales Army, this pub is popular with those who, in ale terms, like to keep it real. Several Camra awards, excellent beer and food.

The Claude, Albany Rd, Roath, **T** 02920 493896. *Mon-Sat 1100-2300, Sun 1100-2230. Map 1, C10, p236* It is unlikely that you will get bored in this popular pub, set in a large traditional building with pool tables, TVs, a juke box, games machines, and even a ten pin bowling alley. As if that's not enough, there's also frequent live music on offer too.

Clubs

The Cameo Club, 3 Pontcanna St, Pontcanna, **T** 02920 220466. *Mon-Thu 0900-0100, Fri, Sat 0900-0200, Sun 1100-2230. Map 1, D7, p236* This private members' club is a favoured haunt of Cardiff's media mafia, but non members can usually get in before

Café-bar society
New, shiny bars are springing up in Cardiff all the time, to the delight of its trendy young population.

2100 – there's an extra charge. It's got big screen facilities so is popular on match days, and has good selection of food and wine.

Vale of Glamorgan

Bars

Plough and Harrow, Monkash, **T** 01656 890209. *Off B4265 near Nash Point. Mon-Sat 1100-2300, Sun 1100-2230.* Pub that's full of character (it's an old Welsh longhouse with an inglenook fireplace) with a good range of real ales. Serves good food too.

The Bush Inn, St Hilary, Cowbridge, **T** 01446 772745. *Off A48. Mon-Sat 1100-2300, Sun 1100-2230.* This ancient inn is popular with locals as it serves good bar meals and real ales. There's a real fire in winter.

The Vale of Glamorgan, High St, Cowbridge, **T** 01446 772252. *Off A48. Mon-Sat 1100-2300, Sun 1100-2230.* Good traditional pub with real fires, real ales and a good atmosphere.

The Victoria Inn, Sigingstone, **T** 01446 773943. *On B4270 near Cowbridge. Mon-Sat 1100-2300, Sun 1100-2230.* Popular pub serving good bar and restaurant meals. Especially noted for its Sunday lunches.

Swansea (Abertawe) and around

Bars

Café Mambo, 46 The Kingsway, Swansea, **T** 01792 456620. Primarily a restaurant, the bar section is very small yet the atmosphere is very good in this Latino themed bar offering cocktails by the glass or pitcher.

Monkey Café Bar, 13 Castle St, Swansea, **T** 01792 480822, www.monkeycafe.co.uk Cool bar offering DJ nights and live music as well as good pub grub in relaxed surroundings during the day.

No Sign Wine Bar, 56 Wind St, Swansea, **T** 01792 465300. *Mon-Sat 1100-2300, Sun 1100-2230.* One of the oldest bars on Wind St and yet another of Dylan Thomas' old haunts. The warm

! The local beer, Brains SA (Special Ale), is often nicknamed
• Same Again – or sometimes, by those who've indulged a little
too much, Skull Attack.

atmosphere of this café-bar tends to attract an eclectic mix of local drinkers, DT fans and clubbers.

Pitcher and Piano, 59-60 Wind St, **T** 01792 461312, www.pitcher andpiano.com *Mon-Sat 1100-2300, Sun 1100-2230.* Enjoy a pint and the shiny wooden floors while reclining on squashy sofas in this large chain bar.

Clubs

Ellington's at the Duke of York, Princess Way, Swansea, **T** 01792 653830. Jazz and cool blues.

Escape, Northampton Lane, Swansea, **T** 01792 652854, www.escapegroup.com *2200-0400 weekends.* The Balearics come to Swansea Bay in this great barn of a venue hosting a variety of club nights.

The Gower (Gwyr)

Bars

Greyhound Inn, Oldwalls, Llanrhidian, **T** 01792 391027. *Off B4295. Mon-Sat 1100-2300, Sun 1100-2230.* Traditional pub said to serve the best beers on the Gower. Wide selection of real ales, and also serves traditional pub grub.

King's Head, Llangennith, **T** 01792 386212. *Off B4271, western end of Gower. Mon-Sat 1100-2300, Sun 1100-2230.* Good selection of real ales as well as bar meals.

Carmarthen (Caerfyddin) and around

Bars

The Forest Arms, Brechfa, **T** 01267 202339. *Off B4310. Mon-Sat 1100-2300, Sun 1100-2230.* Good pub in the village of Brechfa.

The Plough, Felingwm-uchaf, **T** 01267 290019. *Off B4310. Mon-Sat 1100-2300, Sun 1100-2230.* Real fires and real ales.

The Salutation, Llandeilo, **T** 01558 823325. *Off A476. Mon-Sat 1100-2300, Sun 1100-2230.* Traditional pub serving real ales with live musi: jazz on Tues, folk on Wed, bluegrass on Thu and tunes on the piano on Sat.

Carmarthen Coast

Bars

New Three Mariners, Market St, Laugharne, **T** 1994 427426. *Mon-Sat 1100-2300, Sun 1100-2230.* Established pub now refurbished and part owned by actor Neil Morrissey. Serves bar food too.

Caerphilly and the Valleys

Bars

Aberaman Hotel, Brynheulog Terrace, Aberaman, **T** 01685 874695. *Off A4059 near Aberdare. Mon-Sat 1100-2300, Sun 1100-2230.* Typical valleys pub serving real ales and bar meals.

Capel, Park Place, Gilfach Fargoed, **T** 01443 830272. *Off A469. Mon-Sat 1100-2300, Sun 1100-2230.* Traditional pub serving several real ales.

Falcon Inn, 1 Incline Row, Cwmaman, Aberdare, **T** 01685 873758. *Off A4059. Mon-Sat 1100-2300, Sun 1100-2230.* Popular pub on the riverside. Serves real ales and bar meals.

Glan Taff, Cardiff Rd, Quakers Yard, Treharris, **T** 01443 410822. *Off A470. Mon-Sat 1100-2300, Sun 1100-2230.* Popular inn on the River Taff, serving real ales and good bar meals.

Brecon Beacons National Park

Bars

Hen and Chickens, 7 Flannel St, Abergavenny, **T** 01873 853613. *Food daily 1100-1500, 1900 onwards.* A nice traditional pub with lots of old pictures and fittings. During the day you can get 'doorstep sandwiches' such as beef or beef with dripping for a bargain £2.70, or larger meals for around £5.25. There are also Sunday lunches and live jazz to follow every Sun night as well as folk music every other Tue.

The Lounge, 21a High St, Abergavenny, **T** 01874 611189. *Mon-Wed 1100-2300, Sun 1200-2230.* Newly opened café/bar serving cocktails and coffees and fast becoming a popular new spot with locals.

Auberge, 25 Frogmore St, Abergavenny, **T** 01874 850990. *Mon-Thu 1100-2300, Fri, Sat 1100-1200, Sun 1900-2230.* Contemporary wine bar/café.

Sarah Siddons pub, High St Inferior, Brecon, **T** 01874 610666. *Food 1200-1500.* Refurbished pub that also serves breakfasts, burgers and fish and chips for under £5.

The White Hart, Brecon Road, Crickhowell, **T** 01873 810473. *Off A40. Food 1200-1430, 1800-2130.* 15th-century pub on the edge of Crickhowell town offering traditional pub grub, as well as some veggie dishes.

Cardiff's got a lively entertainment scene, and is particularly good if you like music. Come here and you might find anyone from Bryn Terfel to Robbie Williams. Homegrown bands like the Stereophonics have played here, of course, and it's a good place to keep your eye out for up-and-coming stars. A new opera venue will be the Wales Millennium Centre, due to open in November 2004. There's a smattering of cinemas, a comedy club, and a clutch of theatres showing everything from old-fashioned panto to experimental works. The local press have details of what's happening in the city. Also look out for *Buzz*, a free, informative monthly guide to listings on gigs, galleries, film etc. Information on the arts in Cardiff is available from **T** 0800 389 9496, www.arts4cardiff.co.uk.

Cinema

The Hollywood actor Ioan Gruffudd hails from Cardiff, and Catherine Zeta Jones from nearby Mumbles – then there's the renowned Sir Anthony Hopkins, and up-coming Rhys Ifans and Matthew Rhys. With big names like that, it's not surprising that Wales has an increasingly fertile film scene. There's an excellent film school situated at Caerleon, near Newport, and work is due to start in 2004 on Dragon Studios, a state-of-the-art film studio near Bridgend. Some films are set in Wales, such as the cult film *Human Traffic* (1999) which was set in Cardiff. Welsh locations are also often used as a dramatic backdrop: the sand dunes of Merthyr Mawr in *Lawrence of Arabia* (1962); Raglan Castle in *Time Bandit*s (1981); Caerphilly Castle in *Restoration* (1995), Snowdonia in the 2nd *Tombraider* (2003). A number of big-budget Bollywood films have also been shot at locations in Cardiff, Caerphilly and the Brecon Beacons. In 2004 *The I Inside* should be released, which was shot in Cardiff, and a couple of Hollywood biggies are also going ahead here soon. The Wales Screen Commission website is worth checking out, www.walesscreencommission.co.uk You can see all the usual big-budget films in Cardiff, but it's also got an art-house cinema for those who like something more thoughtful. There's an annual film festival too (see festivals).

Chapter Arts Centre, Market Rd, Canton, **T** 02920 311050, www.chapter.org *Map 1, D7, p236* This popular venue has two cinema screens showing art-house movies and mainstream pictures, as well as many foreign films. It's also got a theatre. Tickets cost around £4.80.

Ster Century Multiplex, Millennium Plaza, **T** 0870 767 2676, www.stercentury.co.uk *Map 2, G4/5, p238* Cardiff's biggest, with 14 screens and state-of-the-art facilities. They also show art-house films on Wed evenings.

UGC, Mary Ann St, **T** 0870 9070 739. *Map 2, H8, p238* Mainstream city-centre multiplex

UCI, Atlantic Wharf, Cardiff Bay, **T** 08706 034 567 2030, www.atlanticwharf-cardiff.com *Map 3, E4, p240* 12-screen multiplex showing almost exclusively mainstream movies.

UCI, Parc Tawe, Swansea, **T** 08700 102030. Swansea's big-budget multi-screen cinema.

Comedy

You can catch some of the biggest names on the stand-up circuit in Cardiff, which has a healthy comedy scene.

The Glee Club, Mermaid Quay, Cardiff Bay, **T** 0870 241 5093, www.glee.co.uk *Map 3, G2, p240* Cardiff's main comedy club regularly stages live acts from comedy circuit regulars. Lee Evans, Mark Steel and Johnny Vegas have strutted their stuff here. Once the acts are over, the laughs continue as the club morphs into a boozy dance venue.

Jongleurs, Millennium Plaza, Wood St, **T** 0870 7870707. *Map 2, G4, p238* The comedy's less edgy than at the Glee, but it's still worth catching. There's also a bar that stays open till late.

Dance

Traditional ballets will generally be staged at the St David's Hall, while more experimental dance might appear at the Chapter Arts Centre or The Point. However, you might also wish to catch some performances of traditional Welsh dance at an eisteddfod or street festival. Several dance festivals are also held in Wales, see the Welsh Folk Dance website, www.welshfolkdance.org.uk.

Music

Wales is known as the land of song, and Cardiff's venues manage to attract a wide variety of big names – from classical to cutting-edge contemporary. Classical music, including the Welsh Proms, is generally staged at the huge St David's Hall, while rock and pop acts play at the big stadiums. Everyone from the Strokes and the Flaming Lips to Shirley Bassey and Tom Jones has played in Cardiff. You can also find jazz, folk (often in pubs) and, of course, traditional Welsh Male Voice Choirs who hold open rehearsals. When the Wales Millennium Centre opens in November 2004 it will be the main venue in Wales for opera, as well as many other arts events. For more information about the welsh folk scene get hold of *Taplas*, a bi-monthly guide, also found online at www.taplas.co.uk.

Barfly Club, Kingsway, **T** 02920 667658, www.barflyclub.com *Map 2, E7, p238* This bar hosts a wide range of live bands, both local and visiting. Chance to see bands that are on their way up. Check gig guides in local press or chance it and see.

Cardiff Coal Exchange, Mount Stuart Square, Cardiff Bay, **T** 02920 494917, www.coalexchange.co.uk *Map 3, E2, p240* The former commercial centre is now a hub for live performances, and hosts the Welsh Music Awards. If it's been good enough for Jools Holland and Van Morrison...

Cardiff International Arena, Mary Ann St, **T** 02920 224488, www.uk.cc/com/cia *Map 2, H9, p238* The prime venue for big-name rock and pop acts: past performers at these venues have included Atomic Kitten, Tom Jones, Blue, Iron Maiden, Holiday on Ice, The Strokes, Robbie Williams and the Stereophonics – so pretty varied. Prices upwards of £20, depending on the act.

Millennium Stadium, Westgate St, **T** 02920 822228. *Map 2, G4, p238* Occasionally plays host to the same kind of acts as the International Arena.

Clwb Ifor Bach and **Toucan Club** (see Bars and clubs, page 143) both have live music worth checking out.

St David's Hall, The Hayes, **T** 02920 878444, www.stdavidshallcardiff.co.uk *Map 2, F7, p238* This huge concert hall dominates much of the city centre. It's the prime venue for classical concerts as well as the Welsh Proms (www.welshproms.co.uk) and other large scale events.

The Pop Factory, Jenkins St, Porth, **T** 01443 688500, www.thepopfactory.com *Off A4058 near Pontypridd.* Good place to catch Welsh rock acts and new Valleys talent.

University Student's Union, Park Place, Cathays Park, **T** 02920 781458, www.cardiff.ac.uk *Map 2, B8, p238* Many events are restricted to NUS card-holders but others are open. Attracts a wide range of big-name bands and dance acts such as Catatonia, The Stereophonics, Travis, Coldplay, and many more.

Wales Millennium Centre, Cardiff Bay, **T** 08700 402000. *Map 3, G4, p240* At time of press, they're still building this arts venue, part of the new face Cardiff is presenting to the world. Opening November 2004 for everything from opera and ballet to musicals.

Jazz

Café Jazz, Sandringham Hotel, St Mary St, **T** 02920 387026, www.cafejazzcardiff.com *Map 2, G6, p238* Home to the Welsh Jazz Society and hosts top local performers as well as international acts. Admission costs depend on acts – call ahead to check.

Male voice choirs

Cardiff Male Voice Choir, rehearses at Cowbridge Rd Methodist Church, Canton on Wed and Fri 1930-2130, **T** 02920 594497 – check beforehand.

Brecon, Llanfaes Primary School, **T** 01874 624776. Rehearsal night is Fri 1930-2100, visitors are welcome (not in Aug):

Talgarth Male Voice Choir, Gwemyfed Rugby Club, Talgarth, **T** 01874 625865. Rehearsal night is Mon 2000-2200 (not late Jul or Aug).

Ystradgynlais Male Voice Choir, Coronation Club, Glanrhyd, Ystradgynlais, **T** 01639 843845. Rehearsal nights are Wed and Fri, 1900-2100.

Theatre

Cardiff's got a thriving theatre scene, and you can see anything from amateur productions and contemporary alternative pieces to crowd-pleasing musicals. This is the place to come to catch new works by Welsh writers.

Chapter Arts Centre, Market Rd, Canton, **T** 02920 311050, box office 02920 304400, www.chapter.org (see cinema). *Map 1, D7, p236* Home to several experimental theatre companies, and offers actors' workshops as well as an eclectic range of full performance pieces. Very lively programme.

New Theatre, Park Place, **T** 02920 878889, www.newtheatrecardiff.com *Map 2, D9, p238* Traditional Edwardian theatre offers everything from opera, ballet, musicals and drama to the odd pantomime at Christmas. It's currently home to the Welsh National Opera (www.wno.org.uk) who will move to the Bay when their new venue is completed.

Norwegian Church Arts Centre, Harbour Dr, Cardiff Bay, **T** 02920 454899, norwegian.church@talk21.com *Map 3, H3, p240* Daily 0900-1700, plus evenings for performances. This attractive little church, where author Roald Dahl was christened, is the venue for all manner of exhibitions, workshops and concerts. Also has a good café.

Sherman Theatre, Senghennydd Rd, **T** 02920 646900, www.shermantheatre.co.uk *Map 2, B9, p238* Concentrates on more serious drama, programmes for children and avant-garde productions. Welsh and English language productions here.

The Point, Mount Stuart Sq, Cardiff Bay, **T** 02920 499979, www.thepointcardiffbay.com *Map 3, F2, p240* This converted church is used to host experimental theatre as well as dance and live music.

Swansea Grand Theatre, Singleton St, Swansea, **T** 01792 475715. Drama, pantomime, opera, ballet, concerts.

Taliesin Arts Centre, University of Wales, Mumbles Rd, Swansea, **T** 01792 236883, www.taliesinartscentre.co.uk Owned and managed by the University of Wales Swansea, the centre is named after Taliesin, the 6th-century Celtic bard, and is home to a wide variety of performances, exhibitions, activities and events, with a cinema, gallery and conference facilities.

Theatre Brycheiniog, Canal Wharf, Brecon, **T** 01874 611622, www.theatrebrycheiniog.co.uk Stages a wide range of concerts, dance, opera and plays.

Wales is famous for its 'eisteddfodau', the singular of which is eisteddfod – a meeting of bards. They take place all over the country and range in size from small local gatherings to major events. There are competitions and poetry; dance, debate and music all feature; and there is an emphasis on the Welsh language. The biggest event of all is the National Eisteddfod which is held annually, alternating between venues in North and South Wales. Druid-like Bardic dress is worn. Other eisteddfodau include the Urdd National Eisteddfod, aimed at young people, which is due to be held in Cardiff in 2005 (www.urdd.org).

February

Celtic Festival of Wales, Vale of Glamorgan, **T** 01656 782103. Celtic music and dance festival.

March

Three Peaks Challenge, Brecon Beacons National Park, **T** 02920 238576. Annual sporting challenge over three main peaks around Abergavenny.

May

Hay festival, Hay-on-Wye, **T** 01497 821217, www.hayfestival.co.uk This internationally known literary festival attracts all the big names in the literary world, as well as celebs hoping to drum up interest in their books: past speakers have included Bill Bryson – and Bill Clinton.

Tredegar House Festival Newport Folk music and dance.

June

Cardiff Singer of the World, www.bbc.co.uk/cardiffsinger BBC Wales' biennial singing competition, usually held in the St David's Hall.

International Festival of Musical Theatre Biennial event alternating with the Singer of the World competition.

Swansea Bay Summer Festival, www.swanseabayfestival.net Events run through the summer months May-Sep.

Gwyl Ifan Major dance festival with events in various locations in Cardiff and at the Museum of Welsh Life, St Fagans.

July

International Storytelling Festival (1st weekend), St Donat's Castle, Vale of Glamorgan, **T** 01446 799100, www.byondtheborder.com

Cardiff Festival (late Jul, early Aug), **T** 02920 872087, www.cardiff-festival.com Annual free arts festival aiming to be the new Edinburgh Festival, with theatre, music, street entertainment, a food fest and fairground. The city's festival culminates in the Big Weekend.

National Eisteddfod of Wales (31 Jul-7 Aug) The national eisteddfod of 2004, Wales' most important cultural gathering, will be held in Newport at Tredegar Park, **T** 02920 803360, www.eisteddfod.org.uk. In 2005 it is due to be held in Caernarfon and in 2006 in Swansea.

August

Brecon Jazz Festival, Brecon, **T** 01874 625557, www.breconjazz.co.uk International jazz festival attracting all the great names in jazz over the years.

September

Cardiff Mardi Gras (end Aug or beginning Sep), **T** 02920 652525, www.cardiffmardigras.co.uk/www.gaywales.co.uk This is a lively lesbian and gay festival which includes dance, music, stalls and information tents.

Festivals and events

Abergavenny Food Festival, **T** 01873 851643, www.abergavennyfoodfestival.co.uk A celebration of the area's local produce, with demonstrations and entertainment.

October

Swansea Festival of Music and the Arts, www.swanseafestival.co.uk Everything from opera to jazz.

Dylan Thomas Festival (27 Oct-9 Nov), Swansea, **T** 01792 463980, www.dylanthomasfestival.org The festival comprises various events held to celebrate the poet and his work, including talks, readings and performances.

November

Cardiff Screen Festival (10-20 Nov 2004), **T** 02920 333300, www.sgrin.co.uk Annual film festival in which over 100 films are screened, many of them European and UK premieres. Welsh-language films and films shot in Wales are also shown. Venues are the Chapter Arts Centre and sometimes the UGC.

Winter Wonderland (end Nov-early Jan), www.cardiff.gov.uk/winterwonderland Cardiff celebrates Christmas and the New Year with an open-air ice rink in front of the City Hall, music and fireworks.

Festivals and events

Festivals and events

Cardiff is an excellent city for shopping. The centre is compact, so you can get around easily on foot, and while there are all the usual high-street chains (Next, Waterstones, HMV, Gap, you name them, they're here), you'll also find a brilliant choice of smaller, specialist outlets selling everything from cigars to guitars. The best places for individual shops are the splendid Victorian and Edwardian arcades, with their glass domes. There are also the usual modern, characterless malls like the huge St David's Centre and Capitol Centre. Pedestrianised Queen Street is the main drag, followed by St Mary Street. Late opening night is Thursday, when most large outlets are open until 2000.

Cardiff

Art/craft

Capsule Gallery, Charles St, **T** 02920 376195. *Map 2, G9, p238* Contemporary art gallery that's a good place to pick up works by up-and-coming Welsh artists.

Craft in the Bay, The Flourish, Lloyd George Ave, Cardiff Bay, **T** 02920 484611. *Open daily. Map 3, F3, p240* Co-operative retail gallery selling eclectic mix of contemporary Welsh furniture, ironwork, ceramics, jewellery and knitwear.

Oriel Makers, 37 Pen-y-Lan Rd, Roath Park, **T** 02920 472595. *Wed-Sat 1000-1700. Map 1, C10, p236* This is a platform for Welsh arts and crafts. Varying exhibitions of work including ceramics, glass, textiles, jewellery and watercolours, most of which is for sale. Work can be commissioned.

The Martin Tinney Gallery, Windsor Place, **T** 02920 641411. *Map 2, D9, p238* Posh gallery for the minted, exhibiting artists like Kyffin Williams and Henry Holland.

Beauty products

Aveda, 7 St Mary St, **T** 02920 233005. *Mon-Fri 0900-1900, Sat 0900-1800. Map 2, F5, p238* Beauty heaven in Cardiff, this specialist Aveda store has all the hair and skin products you can imagine. You can also book for a haircut, facial or body treatment. There's a small healthy café too (see eating).

Honzou Corporation, 28 Castle Arcade, **T** 02920 344111. *Mon-Fri 1030-1700, Sat 1030-1730. Map 2, E6, p238* Great shop specializing in natural cosmetics and organic skin creams from Japan. Also stocks Japanese art and crafts.

Books

Ian Allan, Royal Arcade, **T** 02920 390615. *Mon-Fri 0900-1730, Sat 0900-1700. Map 2, G6, p238* Trainspotter heaven – a specialist train bookshop. It's also got titles on aviation.

Oxfam, 36 St Mary St, **T** 02920 222275. *Mon-Sat 0930-1730, Sun 1100-1600. Map 2, G6, p238* Well-stocked secondhand bookshop, a good place to pick up Welsh titles – and cheap 'speak Welsh in 30 days'-type of guides.

Waterstone's, The Hayes, **T** 02920 665606. *Mon, Wed, Fri 0900-1800, Tue 1000-1730, Thu 0900-1900, Sun 1100-1700. Map 2, G7, p238* Well-known big chain bookshop, with a good choice of Welsh titles.

Clothing

@ Fab, High St Arcade. *Mon-Sat 1000-1730. Map 2, F6, p238* The place to come for women needing a special number – long dresses, pretty bags, etc.

Drooghi, High St Arcade, **T** 02920 230332. *Mon-Sat 1000-1730. Map 2, F6, p238* Cool clothes store for the about-town trendy. Va Va voom.

Hobos, High St Arcade, **T** 02920 341188. *Mon-Sat 1100-1730. Map 2, F6, p238* Great retro shop with large and psychedelic range of 60s and 70s clothes.

Independence Day

Cardiff's arcades provide the antidote to high street big chain shopping.

Pussy Galore, High St Arcade, **T** 02920 312400. *Mon-Sat 1000-1730. Map 2, F6, p238* This unfortunately named shop is packed with women's 'dressing up for the evening' glam clothes.

The Pavilion, Wharton St. *Map 2, G6, p238* Men's clothing store with designer labels like Burberry, Timberland and Lacoste.

Woodenwood, Duke St Arcade, **T** 02920 389592. *Mon-Sat 1000-1730. Map 2, G6, p238* Stocks a range of women's clothing including Chilli Pepper and Fcuk with plans to introduce Gucci and Fendi in the future.

Woodies Emporium, 22-26 Morgan Arcade, **T** 02920 232171. *Mon-Thu 0900-1730, Fri, Sat 0900-1800. Map 2, G6, p238* All sorts of designer labels to covet and drool over, from the likes of Paul Smith and Armani.

Department stores

David Morgan, The Hayes, **T** 02920 221011. *Mon-Wed, Fri 0900-1730, Thu 0900-2000, Sat 0900-1800. Map 2, G7, p238* Cardiff's long-established independent, family-run department store. All you'd expect, from haberdashery to hosiery, and a good selection of quality Welsh gifts.

Howells, St Mary St, **T** 02920 231055. *Mon-Wed, Fri, Sat 0900-1800, Thu 0900-2000, Sun 1100-1700. Map 2, F6, p238* House of Fraser store with everything from perfume to designer clothing. Handy toilets on the second floor, and a café/restaurant.

Food and drink

Central Market, off St Mary St. *Map 2, F6, p238* This good old-fashioned covered market has stalls selling everything from fruit and veg to books. Good place to stock up on fresh bread and Welsh cheese. Huge slabs of cake are also popular.

Blas, Old Library, The Hayes. *Tue-Sat 1000-1600 (see eating). Map 2, F7, p238* This place showcases the best of Welsh food and drink. You can find Danzy Jones (a Welsh whisky liqueur), Cariad wine, Welsh whisky, chocolates, specialist honey and Ty Nant water. Best of all are the cheeses – some mild, some creamy and some laced with chillies or herbs.

Furniture/homewares

Back to my Place, Bridge St, **T** 02920 400800, www.b2mp.com *Tue, Wed, Fri, Sat 1000-1800, Thu 1000-1900, Sun 1100-1700. Map 2, G9, p238* Come here for funky furniture and designer homewares such as Alessi, or the Dutch Pisa Vase goods.

Bo Concept, 43-45 The Hayes, **T** 02920 383831, www.boconcept.co.uk *Mon-Wed, Fri, 0900-1800, Thu 0900-2000, Sat 0830-1800, Sun 1100-1700. Map 2, G7, p238* Specialise in contemporary Danish designer furniture, accessories and glassware. Brands stocked include Menu, Club 8 and Rosendahl.

Custom House, 58 Mount Stuart Sq, Cardiff Bay. *Wed, Thu, Fri 1000-1700. Map 2, E2, p238* Stock contemporary accessories, furnishings and art works.

Melin Tregwynt, Royal Arcade, **T** 02920 224997. *Mon-Sat 1000-1730. Map 2, G6, p238* One of *the* places to shop in Cardiff, with all sorts of Welsh covetables, like fine woollen blankets, contemporary rugs, china and accessories.

Momentum, 31 Charles St, **T** 02920 236266. *Tue-Fri 1000-1730, Sat 1000-1800. Map 2, G9, p238* Four floors of designer homewares and furniture, stocking brands from the likes of Tolomeo, Duna and Artemide.

Jewellery

Silver Studio, Royal Arcade, **T** 02920 397111. *Mon-Sat 1000-1700. Map 2, G6, p238* Come here for contemporary silver jewellery. Not a hint of bling.

Time House Jewellery, Oxford Arcade, **T** 02920 382050. *Mon-Sat 0900-1730. Map 2, G7, p238* This is the place to pick up that Welsh gold wedding ring, or Celtic-style jewellery.

Music

Spillers Records, 36 The Hayes, **T** 02920 224905. *Map 2, G7, p238* Old established record shop that's got a great selection of sounds by Welsh artists.

Shoes

Buzz and Co, High St Arcade, **T** 02920 668788. *Mon-Wed 1000-1730, Fri-Sat 1000-1800. Map 2, F6, p238* Great shop for the shoe fetishist fed up with standard high-street offerings.

Souvenirs

Millennium Stadium, Westgate St, **T** 02920 822228. *Mon-Sat 0930-1700. Map 2, G4, p238* Sells a full range of merchandise, including the official Welsh Rugby and Welsh football strips.

Shop Wales, 9 St John St, **T** 02920 373770. *Mon-Sat 0930-1730, and Sun match days 1100-1600. Map 2, F7, p238* Full to bursting with Welsh souvenirs with which to delight the folks back home.

Recommended retail vice
Shopaholics should find a satisfactory fix in Cardiff's many malls.

Among the T-shirts, baby-gros, mouse mats and blow-up dragons are kilts emblazoned with the Welsh dragon and an enticing range of fly-the-flag underwear. If you know someone who would benefit from a pair of 'Unleash the Dragon' Y-fronts then this is the place to come.

Vale of Glamorgan

Art/crafts

The Market Place, Penny Lane, Cowbridge, Vale of Glamorgan. *Tue-Sat 0930-1630.* Showcases work of local artists and craftspeople – a good place to find anything from a cute little bag to a painting.

Clothing

Goose Island, 50a High St, Cowbridge, **T** 01446 771072, www.goose-island.co.uk *Mon-Sat 1000-1700.* Lovely clothes from the Far East, as well as bags, jewellery and gifts.

McArthur Glen Designer Outlet Retail Park aka The Pines, www.mcarthurglen.com *Off J36 off M4 near Bridgend. Mon-Fri 1000-2000, Sat 1000-1800, Sun 1100-1700.* Has about 80 designer outlet stores, up to 50% off RRP, spend at least half a day here to see round it all.

Furniture/homewares

Xantippe, High St, Cowbridge. Posh French and European painted furniture.

Swansea and the Gower

Art/craft

Attic Gallery, 14 Cambrian Place, Swansea, **T** 01792 653387, www.atticgallery.co.uk *Tue-Fri 1000-1730, Sat 1000-1630*. A good place for buying contemporary Welsh art.

Souvenirs

The Lovespoon Gallery, 492 Mumbles Rd, Mumbles, **T** 01792 360132. *Mon–Sat 1000-1730*. Lovespoons are traditional hand-carved spoons given to lovers.

Surfing gear

Surf and Snow, Castleton Arcade, Mumbles, **T** 01792 363169. *Daily 0900-1300, 1330-1730*. New and used boards and wetsuits.

Hot Dog Surf Shop, Kittle, The Gower, **T** 01792 234073, *Daily 0930-1800*. More surfing goodies.

Hay-on-Wye

Books

With 39 bookshops for the population of 1300 in Hay-on-Wye and an annual festival, Hay-on-Wye is the book capital of the UK. See Festivals and events for details of the annual ten-day Hay Festival and for full listings of bookshops in the town, consult the official website www.hay-on-wye-co.uk

Richard Booth, 44 Lion St, **T** 01497 820322, www.richardbooth.demon.co.uk. The man and shop that started it all. Largest bookshop in Hay selling all manner of second hand titles. Richard's wife runs the bookshop at Hay Castle.

Marijana Dworski, 21 Broad St, **T** 01497 820 200. Second hand travel, culture and history books covering the Balkans, Europe, Russia and Central Asia. Plus dictionaries and books on over 250 of the world's languages.

Hay Cinema Bookshop, The Old Cinema, **T** 01497 820071. Bookshop covering all subjects housed in the converted cinema.

Boz Books, 13A Castle St, **T** 01497 821277. General bookshop specializing in 19th century English literature. The place to find Charles Dickens first editions, as well as some 20th century welsh writing from the likes of Dylan Thomas.

Deborah Harding Books, The Broad Street Book Centre, 6 Broad St, **T** 01497 821919. New and second hand books covering the mind, body and soul genre – including spirituality, psychoanalysis, mythology, arts and crafts and other touchy-feeling themes.

Cardiff's the ideal city for lovers of the outdoors. From here you can easily reach the Brecon Beacons National Park, with its rugged mountain ranges, or make for some of the superb surfing beaches that etch the nearby coastline. One of the favourite beaches for surf aficionados is Llangennith on the Gower, or you can try your hand at kite surfing, currently the hottest thing in watersports. You name it, you can do it here: riding, climbing, mountain biking, sailing, canoeing, bird-watching. If you fancy more of an adrenalin rush then there's always paragliding.

If you're happiest in boots and a woolly hat, there are several long-distance walking paths within easy reach of Cardiff. One of the best known is the Offa's Dyke Path, a 178-mile journey running from the Severn Estuary in Chepstow to the northern coast near Prestatyn. Other paths include the Pembrokeshire Coast Path (186 miles of spectacular cliff-top scenery), the Wye Valley Walk (144 miles), the Dyfi Valley Way (108 miles) and the Severn Valley Way (210 miles). A useful website is www.activitywales.com.

Cardiff

Cycling

Taff Trail Cycle Hire Centre, off Cathedral Rd, near the Cardiff Caravan Park and by Pontcanna Fields, **T** 02920 39 8362. Bikes are available for day rental from £9.45 for adults, £7.05 for children; shorter rents also possible, £28 for a family ticket (2 adults and 2 children). Bikes for disabled people available from £2 per hr, pre-booking essential. The Taff Trail extends from Cardiff Bay to Brecon, 87km (54 miles) to the north.

Football

Cardiff City FC, play at Ninian Park, Ninian Park Rd, **T** 02920 221001, www.cardiffcityfc.co.uk

Golf

Bridgend Golf Complex, Bridgend, **T** 01656 647926. *Off A48*. Nine-hole pay and play course, floodlit driving range.

Health and beauty

St David's Hotel and Spa, Havannah St, **T** 02920 454045, www.roccofortehotels.com *Cardiff Bay*. Voted third best UK spa by Conde Nast Traveller readers, the spa at Cardiff's five-star hotel is open to non residents seeking some serious pampering. It's a hydrotherapy spa with an exercise pool, sauna and yoga studio and also has treatment rooms where you can have aromatherapy or hydrotherapy massages, get your chakras sorted out and generally chill. Day packages cost from £65.

▶ Playing for kicks

Rugby, Wales' flagship sport, has taken a battering. The glory days of the 70s, when the Welsh game basked in the glory of players like Gareth Edwards and JPR Williams, are well over.

The bell began to toll for Welsh rugby with the arrival of professionalism in 1995. Once the game became a business, something of its gutsy spirit was lost, and Wales found it hard to find a foothold in this acquisitive commercial world.

Although hugely popular throughout the country, the notion of Wales as a rugby nation was never entirely accurate. In terms of clubs and top players, the game was pretty much the preserve of the industrialised south. In the rural north, soccer, an import from nearby Liverpool and Manchester, took first place.

The Millennium Stadium, a state-of-the-art venue, constructed bang in the centre of Cardiff, was built to replace the legendary Cardiff Arms Park, scene of many Welsh rugby wins (for 28 years the English side did not win once in Cardiff).

In 1999 the Rugby World Cup was hosted by Wales (the team reached the quarter finals). So far so traditional. But this rugby venue is now also the home of the FA Cup, at least until a replacement for Wembley Stadium is up and running.

So football versus rugby? Chances are the two passions will run side by side, just as they always have.

And on a positive note, Welsh Women's Rugby is still flying the flag with a good deal of success. For further information look up www.wru.co.uk.

Ice hockey

The Ice House, Hayes Bridge, **T** 02920 397198, www.thecardiffdevils.com This ice rink is home to the Cardiff Devils, Wales' main ice hockey team.

Rugby

The Millennium Stadium, Westgate St, **T** 02920 822228, www.millenniumstadium.co.uk *The* sporting venue in Wales, and the home of Welsh rugby (www.wru.co.uk).

Cardiff Rugby Club, **T** 02920 302000, www.cardiffrfc.com, play at the Arms Park, Westgate St, by the Millennium Stadium.

Swansea (Abertawe) and around

Cycling

The Millennium Coastal Park has a 20-km cycle trail along the Loughor Estuary and runs from Bynea in the east to Pembury in the west. It offers traffic-free, family-friendly cycling.

Pedalabikeaway, North Dock, Llanelli, **T** 01554 780123, www.pedalabikeaway.com Loads of bikes for hire, from mountain bikes to tandems.

Schmoos Cycles, Lower Oxford St, Swansea, **T** 01792 410710. Cycle hire.

Swansea Cycles, 10 Wyndham St, Swansea, **T** 01792 410710. Cycle hire: half day £8, full day £14.

Golf

Clyne Golf Club, Mayals, Swansea, **T** 01792 40198, www.clynegolfclub.com 18-hole course on undulating ground.

Having a ball
Neil Jenkins played fly half for Wales during the 1990s and scored more than 1000 points for his country.

Earlswood Golf, Swansea, **T** 01792 321578. 18-hole pay and play course, green fees £9 per round.

Swansea Bay Golf Club, Neath, **T** 01792 812198. 18-hole, par 72 links course.

The Gower (Gwyr)

Riding

Parc le Breos, Parkmill, Gower, **T** 01792 371636, www.parc-le-breos.co.uk Daily rides and pony trekking holidays.

Pitton Moor Trekking, Pilton Cross, Rhossili, Gower, **T** 01792 390554. WTRA-approved trekking on the Gower.

Walking

Gower Guided Walks, **T** 01792 652040, www.gower guidedwalks.co.uk Variety of guided walks on the Gower.

Watersports

Bay Watersports, Oystermouth Rd, **T** 01792 534858, www.baywatersports.co.uk Offer windsurfing lessons and kit hire. One lesson £20, two-day course (four lessons) £65.

Euphoria Sailing, Oxwich Bay, **T** 0870 7702890 or 07812 774701, www.watersports4all.com Offer a variety of watersports in Oxwich Bay, from sailing and windsurfing to wakeboarding.

PJs Surf Shop, Llangennith, Gower, **T** 01792 386669, www.pjsurfshop.co.uk. Good range of wetsuits and surfboards for hire (from £9); also have a surf hotline, **T** 0901 603 1603 (60p per minute).

Welsh Surf School, Llangennith, Gower, **T** 01792 386426, www.wsfsurfschool.co.uk Run surfing lessons from Apr-Oct in Rhossili Bay (Llangennith).

Monmouthshire

Canoeing

Monmouth Canoe and Activity Centre, Castle Yard, Monmouth, **T** 01600 713461, www.monmouthcanoehire.20m.com Offer canoe hire and kayaking on the Wye.

Wye Valley Canoes, Glasbury-on-Wye, Herefordshire, **T** 01497 847213, www.wyevalleycanoes.co.uk Over the border in England, offer canoeing and kayaking on the Wye.

Cycling/mountain biking

Pedalabikeaway Cycle Centre, Cannop Valley, near Coleford, **T** 01594 860065, www.pedalabikeaway.com *Just over the border.* Bike hire, maps and information, as well as mountain bike trails.

Pedalaway, Trereece Barn, Llangarron, Ross-on-Wye, **T** 01989 770357, www.pedalaway.co.uk Mountain-bike trails and routes for casual cyclists, range of bikes to hire.

Golf

Celtic Manor Resort, Coldra Woods, Newport, **T** 01633 413000, www.celtic-manor.com/www.walesopen.com This leisure and golf resort/hotel has three championship courses, a golf school and a health club and spa. Will host the Ryder Cup in 2010.

Dewstow Golf Club, Caerwent, **T** 01291 430444, www.dewstow.com Two 18-hole parkland golf courses, floodlit golf range.

Monmouth Golf Club, Leasbrook Lane, Monmouth, **T** 01600 712212, www.monmouthgolfclub.co.uk Parkland golf course.

Shirenewton Golf and Country Club, Shirenewton, **T** 01291 641642. 18-hole golf course, green fees from £16.

Caerphilly and the Valleys

Climbing

Welsh International Climbing Centre, Taff Bargoed Centre, Trelewis, Treharris, **T** 01443 710749, www.indoorclimbingwalls.co.uk. *South of Merthyr Tydfil*. Offers indoor climbing (largest indoor climbing wall in Europe), caving, abseiling, high ropes courses and mountain bike hire – two-hr and half-day introductory tasters, adult lessons and longer breaks. Also have bunkhouse accommodation.

Cycling/mountain biking

National Cycle Route runs from Blaenavon through Pontypool and into Cwmbran, using old railway lines and canal towpath as far as possible. Further Details from **Countryside Section**, *Development Department, Floor 4, County Hall, Cwmbran, NP44 2WN*, **T** *01633 648034.*

A selection of walks

The Severn Way: 210 miles (337 km), www.severnway.com Traces the course of the River Severn from its source on Plynlimon to the Bristol Channel. 55 miles of the route are in Powys.

Offa's Dyke Path: 182 miles (293 km), **T** 01547 528753, oda@offasdyke.demon.co.uk Follows, as far as possible, the line of Offa's Dyke from Prestatyn to Chepstow, along the border of England and Wales. It runs through Knighton and passes very close to Montgomery and Welshpool.

The Wye Valley Walk: 136 miles (218 km), **T** 01597 827567(for Powys section) , www.wyevalleywalk.org Follows the river valley from Chepstow to the Plynlimon mountains. Passes through Builth Wells and Rhayader.

Monnow Valley Walk: 40 miles (63.5 km) Hay-on-Wye to Monmouth, guidebook from (and by) Eira and Harry Steggles, Treffynon, Lower Prospect Rd, Monmouth, NP25 3HS.

Three Castles Walk: 19 miles (30.5 km) Links castles at Grosmont, Skenfrith and White Castle, guidebook from Monmouthshire County Council.

Coed Morgannwg Way: 36 miles (58 km) Follows forest tracks from Gethin Woodland Park near Merthyr Tydfil

Cwmcarn Forest Drive, Visitor Centre and Campsite, Cwmcarn, Crosskeys, **T** 01495 272001, cwmcarn-vc@caerphilly-gov.uk, www.caerphilly.gov.uk/visiting Mountain biking track, the Twrch Trail, in former coal mining area. There is also a visitor centre, forest drive (£3 charge per car), guided and self-guided walks, and a campsite.

to Margam, near Neath, guide published by Neath and Port Talbot County Borough Council.

Millennium Heritage Trail: 72 miles (116 km) A circular walking route from St Fagans and around the villages and towns of the Vale of Glamorgan. Information from Valeways, Unit 7 Barry Enterprise Centre, Skomer Rd, Barry, Vale of Glamorgan, CF62 9DA, **T** 01446 749000.

Wye Valley Walk: 136 miles (218 km), www.wyevalley walk.org From Chepstow to Plynlimon in Powys. The walk takes you through some lovely pastoral landscapes – including Tintern Abbey – and passes several market towns, such as Monmouth, Ross-on-Wye and Hay-on-Wye. An official route guide is available from Wye Valley AONB Office, Hadnock Rd, Monmouth, **T** 01600 710846, costing approximately £9 including p&p.

Cambrian Way: 274 miles (441 km), www.cambrian way.com The longest and toughest path from Cardiff to Conwy via Snowdon – consult the guidebook by Tony Drake, available from the Ramblers Association.

General information – www.walking.visitwales.com Information on Walking in Wales from Ramblers' Association, 1 Cathedral Rd, Cardiff, CF11 9HA, **T** 02920 343535.

Golf

Rhondda Golf Club, Golf House, Penrhys, Ferndale, **T** 01443 442384. 18-hole Valleys Mountain course.

Riding

Groeswen Riding Stables, Ty Canol Farm, Caerphilly, **T** 02920 880500, www.groeswenstables.com Escorted trekking from one-hr to full day.

Brecon Beacons National Park

Brecon Beacons Mountain Centre, Libanus, **T** 01874 623366, www.breconbeacons.org *6 miles from Brecon off A470. Daily Mar-June, Sept, Oct 0930-1700, July, Aug 0930-1800, Nov-Feb 0930-1630, free.* This centre has plenty of maps, guides and information on outdoor activities in the area and is a good starting point for walks, whether gentle or challenging. There's a good café and an exhibition on the National Park.

General outdoor activities

Black Mountain Activities, Three Cocks, near Hay on Wye, **T** 01497 847897, www.blackmountain.co.uk One- to five-day multi-activity breaks, with white water rafting, mountain biking, caving etc. Mountain bike and canoe hire.

Mountain and Water, 2 Uppe Cwm, Nant Gam, Llanelli Hill, **T** 01873 831825, www.mountainandwater.co.uk All sorts of activities including abseiling, coasteering and caving. Days, holidays and courses.

Watersports

Brecon Boats, Travellers Rest Inn, Talybont on Usk, **T** 01874 676401. Self-drive boat hire on Monmouthshire to Brecon Canal.

Celtic Canoes, Newport St, Hay-on-Wye, **T** 01497 847422, www.canoehireuk.com Offers canadian canoe hire, instruction and tours.

Llangorse Lake, near Brecon, www.brecon-beacons.com/llangorse-lake The lake is a general outdoor activity area and is good for sailing, rowing, canoeing or fishing. Camping available at

Lakeside, **T** 01874 658226, www.lakeside-holidays.net **PGL Llangorse Sailing School**, **T** 01874 658657; **Llangorse Sailing Club**, **T** 01874 658596.

Monmouthshire and Brecon Canal, near Rich Way, Brecon, **T** 07831 685222, www.dragonfly-cruises.co.uk 2½-hr cruise on the Dragonfly canal boat , £5, Mar-end Oct, twice daily.

Paddles and Pedals, 15 Castle St, Hay-on-Wye, **T** 01497 820604, www.canoehire.co.uk Canoe and kayak hire.

Wye Valley Canoes, The Boat House, Glasbury-on-Wye, Hereford, **T** 01497 847213, www.wyevalleycanoes.co.uk Canoeing on the Wye, suitable for families.

Sports

Caving

Good caves for beginners are **Porth yr Ogof**, near Ystradfellte, and **Chartist Cave** on the Llangyndir Moors. Permission is needed and you should go as part of a group/course. Specialist shop is **Crickhowell Adventure Sports**, **T** 01873 810020. More on caving from www.caving.uk.com Operators include the **Robert Jeffery Centre**, Abergavenny, **T** 01873 831185.

Climbing

Llangorse Rope Centre, Gilfach Farm, Llangorse, **T** 01874 658272, www.activityuk.com Indoor climbing centre with natural rock faces, climbing walls and facilities for kids. Also do range of other activities including horse riding. Open Mon-Sat 0930-2200, Sun 0930-1800, two-hour climbing/acitivity session £13, one-hour climbing taster £11; trekking from £11 for an hour to £32 for a full day for beginners. Also has bunkhouse accommodation.

Cycling/mountain biking

Brecon Cycle Centre, 10 Ship St, **T** 01874 622651, www.breconcycles.com Bicycle hire.

Pedalaway, Hopyard Farm, Govilon, near Abergavenny, **T** 01873 830219, www.pedalaway.co.uk Bikes for hire.

Golf

Brecon Golf Club, Newton Park, Llanfaes, **T** 01874 622004. Nine-hole flat parkland course, green fee £12.

Cradoc Golf Club and Driving Range, Penoyre Park, Cradoc, **T** 01874 623658, www.cradoc.co.uk 18-hole parkland golf course and floodlit driving range.

Wernddu Golf Centre, Abergavenny, **T** 01873 856223. 18-hole course and pitch and putt, camping available.

Mountaineering

Kevin Walker Mountain Activities, 74 Beacons Park, **T** 01874 625111. Runs mountain craft, climbing and caving courses in the Brecon Beacons.

Paragliding

Blorenge mountain near Abergavenny is a popular area for paragliding. Information from **Welsh Hang Gliding and Paragliding Centre**, **T** 01873 850910, www.hg-pg.com

Riding

Cantref Riding Centre, Upper Cantref Farm, Cantref, **T** 01874 665223, www.cantref.com Offer everything from one-hour to full-day rides on the Brecon Beacons.

Grange Trekking Centre, Capel-y-Ffin, near Abergavenny, **T** 01873 890215. Trekking holidays in the Black Mountains. Apr-Oct.

Llanthony Riding and Trekking, Court Farm, Llanthony, **T** 01873 890359, www.llanthony.co.uk *Apr-Oct*. Trekking for beginners and hacks for more experienced riders.

Mills Bros, Newcourt Farm, Felindre, Three Cocks, **T** 01497 847285. Half- and full-day treks in the Black Mountains.

Tregoyd Mountain Rides, Three Cocks, near Hay-on-Wye, **T** 01497 847351, www.tregoydriding.co.uk Hourly or full-day rides and treks. Accommodation available.

Wern Riding Centre, Llangattock Hillside, Crickhowell, **T** 01873 810899, www.wiz.to/wern *Apr-Oct*. A range of trekking, hacking and trail-riding options.

Cardiff is the most cosmopolitan city in Wales, so not surprisingly has the liveliest and most confident gay scene. It's not as large or well established as those in cities like London, Manchester or Edinburgh, but is certainly growing. In 1999 the first Mardi Gras lesbian and gay pride festival was held here, and it is now an established feature of the city calendar, with dance, music, stalls and information. Most of the gay venues in the city are focused on Charles Street in the city centre. A useful website is www.gaywales.co.uk

Bars and clubs

Bar XS, 35 Charles St, **T** 02920 400876. *Daily from 1800-2300. Map 2, G9, p238* This is a busy bar above Club X (see clubs). There's a terrace garden and a lively atmosphere – it's packed to the gunnels at weekends and offers good cruising potential.

Club X, 16-39 Charles St, **T** 02920 400876. *Wed-Thu 2200-0200, Fri 2200-0300, Sat 2200-0400. Map 2, G9, p238* Attached to Bar XS, this is a stylish and very popular gay club. Gets extremely busy on Wednesday (student night) and at weekends when there's house music and it's hot and sweaty. You can drink on the terrace on fine summer nights.

Exit, 48 Charles St, **T** 02920 640102. *Mon-Sat 2000-0200, Sun 2000-0030. Map 2, G9, p238* Unlike other gay clubs in Cardiff, this one's more female dominated. There's dancing downstairs and a garden for warm nights.

Golden Cross, 283 Hayes Bridge Rd, **T** 02920 394556. *Open from 1200 daily. Map 2, H7, p238* This restored Victorian pub is extremely popular – it's quieter during the day but a lively party atmosphere reigns at night, when it's largely male dominated. Lots of camp entertainment – from cabaret to karaoke – and a good place for Sunday lunch too.

KX, Mill Lane, **T** 02920 649891. *Happy hour from 1700-2000 Mon-Thu. Mon-Thu 1200-2300, Fri, Sat 1200-0100, Sun 1200-0030. Map 2, H7, p238* Long-established gay bar (formerly King's Cross) that's lively, mixed every night and has plenty of special events, varying from Wed cabaret, Thu School disco, Fri and Sat House Party and drag queen Miss Kitty's Karaoke on Sun.

Lush, 22 Caroline St, **T** 02920 359123. *Mon-Fri 1500-2400, Sat 1300-2400, Sun 1700-1230.* Chilled gay-owned wine bar in the city centre.

Saviour, @Gretsky's, The Academy Ice Rink, Hayes Bridge Rd, *Opposite the Golden Cross. Opens 2200, £5 admission, every other week on a Sat. Map 2, H7, p238* Cardiff's newest gay club, with two separate rooms pumping out different music, bars, go-go dancers and drag acts.

Saunas

Locker Room, 50 Charles St, **T** 02920 220388. *Sun-Fri 1300-2300, Sat 1300-1800, Entry £11, day membership £1. Map 2, g9, p238* Popular friendly gay men's sauna that's also got a jacuzzi and steam room.

Cardiff's got plenty to interest kids, with even 'serious' attractions like the National Museum of Wales having a techno-style section on the Evolution of Wales (page 43) that is very child-friendly. And the interiors in the Castle are wacky enough to arouse interest in all but the most sulky of teenagers. Down in the Bay you can get the whole family out on a high-speed boat trip or, if you've got smaller kids, you can take them out to popular Roath Park to see the swans on the lake. For energetic youngsters needing to let off steam there are simply loads of places to go in the areas surrounding the city. The Brecon Beacons offers almost infinite possibilities, while the whole family can go canoeing on the Wye, or just enjoy a day on the beach in the Gower. There are a reasonable number of child-friendly places to eat – and the great advantage of a city surrounded by so much open space is that there are loads of potential picnic spots.

Places for kids

- Millennium Stadium, p42
- Techniquest, p50
- Boat trip on Cardiff Bay, p54
- Museum of Welsh Life, p57
- Big Pit, Blaenavon, p89

Britain still lags some way behind southern Europe in its attitude towards young children, and unlike their Mediterranean cousins, most British citizens are unlikely to feel better disposed towards foreign visitors travelling with kids in tow. There are however, lots of attractions geared towards childre, so finding something to keep the ankle-biters amused while the rain tips down shouldn't be a problem. The most frustrating aspect of travelling with kids in Britain is eating out. Some establishments are happy to help with high chairs and kids' menus while too many are downright unhelpful. Italian restaurants are often more child-friendly. In more remote areas, however, most people are helpful and friendly.

● *www.babygoes2.com is a very useful source of advice.*

Sights

Museum of Welsh Life, St Fagans, **T** 02920 573500. *Bus 32 or 320, about every hour from city centre, less frequent on Sun. Taxis cost around £10. Daily 1000-1700, free. Map 1, C1, p236* This excellent open-air museum could easily take up a full day. It covers around 44 acres (18 ha) of ground in which have been rebuilt a collection of 40 period Welsh buildings, taken from all over the country – so you can wander into an early farmhouse, see an old Welsh school, or walk along a terrace of miner's cottages, some complete with outside toilets, always a favourite with kids. There's an old shop and working bakery too.

Techniquest, Stuart St, Cardiff Bay, **T** 02920 475475, www.techniquest.org *Mon-Fri 0930-1630, Sat, Sun 1030-1700, school holidays Mon-Fri 0930-1700. £6.75 adults, £4.65 children, £18.50 family. Map 3, G1, p240* At this interactive science centre fun and education come together. You can have a go at a load of 'hands-on' exhibits – firing a rocket, perhaps – or look at more serious exhibits on building a dam. There's a planetarium, and, at weekends and during holidays, demonstrations are held in the Science Theatre.

The Millennium Stadium, Westgate St, **T** 02920 822228, www.millenniumstadium.co.uk *Shop open Mon-Sat 0930-1700, tours 1000-1700 run hourly on the hour, booking advised and subject to events, go to Gate 3 on Westgate St. £5 adults, £2.50 children, £3 conc, £15 family. Map 2, G4, p238* This should please the rugby and footie fans, a tour of the top sporting venue in Wales. It's the home of Welsh rugby and hosts matches in the annual Six Nations Championships rugby, as well as international football matches. If you go on a tour you'll be shown the dressing rooms, the tunnel, and the pitch – alternatively you could just bring them here to watch a game.

Around Cardiff

Big Pit National Mining Museum, Blaenavon, **T** 01495 790311, www.nmgw.ac.uk *Approx 1 mile west of Blaenavon. mid Feb-end Nov daily 0930-1700, 1st tour 1000, last 1530. Free.* Historic mine that gives an excellent insight into the life of the Valleys' coal miners. A tour takes you 3,000 ft (90 m) underground. You don a helmet, cap-lamp and battery pack and, guided by ex-miners, go down to the coal face. (Not for tiny children)

Llancaiach Fawr Manor, Nelson, **T** 01443 412248. *On B4254 near Nelson, north of Caerphilly. Mar-end Oct Mon-Fri 1000-1700,*

Sat, *Sun 1000-1800, closed Mon Nov-Feb. £4.50 adults, £3 children, £12 family.* Manor house that is now a living history museum. It focuses on the year 1645 – the Civil War – and has guides dressed in period clothing.

Margam Park, Margam, near Port Talbot, **T** 01639 881635, www.neath-porttalbot .gov.uk/margampark *Reached by junction 38, M4. Daily Easter-end Sep 1000-1730, winter 1000-1630. Free, £2 car park.* Delightful parkland surrounding an elaborate 19th-century house and the romantic ruins of Margam Abbey. It's fairly low key, in that there are lots of bells and whistles attractions but it's an extensive area with deer in the parkland, a walled garden, and a play area for children.

Sports

Llangorse Rope Centre, Gilfach Farm, Llangorse, **T** 01874 658272, www.activityuk.com *Open Mon-Sat 0930-2200, Sun 0930-1800.* Indoor climbing centre with natural rock faces, climbing walls and facilities for kids. Also do range of other activities including horse riding.

Welsh International Climbing Centre, Taff Bargoed Centre, Trelewis, Treharris, **T** 01443 710749, www.indoorclimbing walls.co.uk *South of Merthyr Tydfil. Open daily.* Offers indoor climbing (largest indoor climbing wall in Europe), and mountain bike hire – two-hr and half-day introductory tasters.

Eating

£ **Harry Ramsden**, Stuart St, Cardiff Bay, **T** 02920 463334. *Mon-Sat 1130-2300, Sun 1130-2130. Map 3, G1, p240* Reliable, child-friendly, fish and chips and peas – one of a great chain that's grown from the original in Yorkshire.

£ **Old Orleans**, 17 Church St, **T** 02920 222078. *Mon-Sun 1200-2300. Map 2, F6, p238* American-style 'we're glad to see the kids' sort of diner – burgers, chips, chicken, sauce.

£ **Verdi's Knab Rock**, Mumbles Rd, **T** 01792 369135, www.verdis-café.co.uk *Daily 1000-2100 (2200 Jul and Aug), earlier closing Mon-Thu in winter.* Relaxed Italian ice cream parlour where you can sit outside on the decking and eat huge ice cream sundaes or pizzas.

Directory

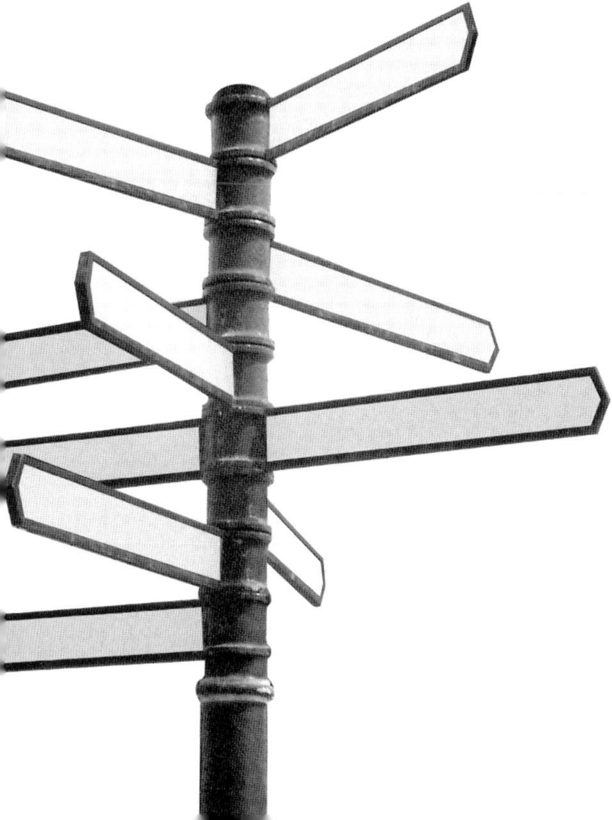

Airline offices

Air Wales, **T** 0870 7773131, www.airwales.co.uk **BMI baby**, **T** 0870 264 2229, www.bmibaby.com **KLM**, **T** 08705 074074, www.klm.com **Ryanair**, **T** 0871 246 0000 or 0871 246 0016, www.ryanair.com.

Banks and ATMs

Bank opening hours are Mon-Fri from around 0930-1600-1700. You can withdraw cash from selected banks and ATMs (cashpoints as they're known in Britain) with your credit/debit card. There is a branch of **Lloyds TSB** on Queen St and other banks can be found there or on High St.

Car hire

Hertz, Cardiff Airport, **T** 01446 711722, www.hertz.co.uk **Europcar**, Cardiff Airport, **T** 01446 711924, www.europcar.com

Currency exchange

Several major banks on Queen St and around the city have exchange, Mon-Fri 0900-1700.

Cultural institutions

Royal Norwegian Consulate, High St, Cowbridge, **T** 01446 774018, www.norway.org.uk Mon-Fri 0900-1730. **American Welsh Affairs Office**, **T** 02920 786633 (no visa or consular services at this branch), London office **T** 0207 499 9000, www.usembassy.org.uk

Dentists

Dentists Riverside Health Centre, Wellington St, Canton, **T** 02920 371221. For emergency (only) dental treatment.

Disabled

Disability Wales, Wernddu Court, Caerphilly Business Park, Van Road, Caerphilly, CF83 3ED, **T** 02920 887325, www.dwac.demon .co.uk Contact for general information. **RADAR**, Head Office 12 City Forum, 250 City Road, London, EC1V 8AF, **T** 0207 2503222, www.radar.org.uk Have information on holidays and travel in the UK. **Traveline Cymru**, **T** 0870 6082608, www.traveline.org.uk Call for details of disabled access on public transport throughout Wales. **Tripscope**, T 0845 7585641, will help any disabled person with their travel plans around the UK. **Wales Council for the Blind**, 3rd Floor, Shand House, 20, Newport Road, Cardiff, CF24 0DB, **T** 02920 473954, www.wcb-ccd.org.uk **Wales Council for the Deaf**, Glenview House, Courthouse Street, Pontypridd, CF37 1JY, **T** 01443 485687, www.wcdeaf.org.uk

Doctors

NHS Wales, T 0845 4647, www.wales.nhs.uk, can offer confidential medical advice over the phone or let you know the location of your nearest doctor. The website also has some useful links for local doctors surgeries and so on. For serious medical emergencies requiring an ambulance, dial **T** 999.

Electricity

The current in Wales is 240V AC. Plugs have three square pins and adapters are widely available.

Embassies

All major embassies are based in London.
Australia, **T** 020 7379 4334; **Canada**, **T** 020 7258 6600; **Denmark**; **T** 020 7235 1255; **France**, **T** 020 7073 1400; **Germany**, **T** 020 7824 1300; **Italy**, **T** 020 7312 2200; **Japan**, **T** 020 7465 6500; **Nether -lands**, **T** 020 7590 3200; **New Zealand**, **T** 020 79308422; **South Africa**, **T** 020 74517299;

Spain, **T** 020 7589 8989; **Sweden**, **T** 020 7917 6400;
Switzerland, **T** 020 7616 6000; **USA**, **T** 020 7499 9000. See also
Cultural Institutions.

Emergency numbers
Police/Fire/Ambulance T 999.
Penarth coastguard T 01792 366534.

Hospitals
University of Wales Hospital, Heath Park, **T** 02920 747747.

Internet/email
Internet Exchange, 8 Church St, **T** 02920 236047. *Mon-Thu
0900-2100, Fri, Sat 0900-2000, Sun 1100-1900.* Non members £1
per 15 mins, day pass £7.

Language schools
Languages Direct, 61 Charles St, **T** 02920 665677. **Cardiff
Language Academy**, 16/17 High St, **T** 02920 226047.

Launderette
Launderama, 60 Lower Cathedral Rd. **Canton Launderette**,
244 Cowbridge Rd East, **T** 02920 341039

Left luggage
Only available at **Cardiff Visitor Centre**, though limited facilities.

Libraries
Cardiff Central Library, Frederick St, **T** 02920 382116. *Mon-Sat
0900-1730.*

Media
The Welsh daily broadsheet is the **Western Mail**, while Cardiff's
regional daily is the **South Wales Echo**. In Swansea you can get

the **Swansea Evening Post**, their regional daily newspaper. On Sundays you can get **Wales on Sunday**. Also look out for **Buzz**, a free local listings magazine that you can get from places like the St David's Hall. All the British national daily and weekend newspapers are available in Wales, including both broadsheets like The Guardian, The Times, The Independent and The Telegraph and tabloids like The Sun, The Mirror and so on.

Pharmacies
There are chemists all over the city. The main one is **Boots**, 36 Queen St, **T** 02920 231291.

Police
Cardiff Police Station, King Edward VIII Avenue, Cathays Park, **T** 02920 222111.

Post offices
Main Post Office, The Hayes. Mon-Fri 090-1730, Sat 0900-1230.

Public holidays
New Year's Day, Good Friday and Easter Monday, May Day (1st Mon in May), Spring Bank Holiday (last Mon in May), August Bank Holiday (last Mon in Aug), Christmas Day (25 Dec) and Boxing Day (26 Dec).

Taxi firms
Black Cab, Riverside, **T** 02920 222999. **Capitol**, **T** 02920 777777, **Castle**, 27 Westgate St, **T** 02920 344344.
Dragon, City Rd, **T** 01633 216216. **Premiere**, **T** 02920 555555/ 02920 565565.

Telephone

Most public payphones are operated by British Telecom (BT) and take either coins (10p, 20p, 50p and £1), credit cards or phonecards, which are available at newsagents and post offices in denominations of £2, £3, £5 and £10. The minimum charge is 20p. Various companies offer cheap international dialling and it is possible to buy international cheap rate cards in most newsagents which can be used in public and private phones.

Transport enquiries
Traveline Wales, **T** 0870 6082608, www.traveline-cymru.org.uk

Travel agents
STA Travel, 11 Duke St, **T** 02920 382350, www.statravel.co.uk and Cardiff University Students Union, Park Place, **T** 02920 389186.

A sprint through history

AD c60-90	Romans build a fort in Cardiff. In 78 AD they complete their conquest of Wales by slaughtering the Druids of Anglesey.
c500	St David's Cathedral founded.
c784	Offa's Dyke is built by Offa, King of Mercia.
c844-878	Prince Rhodri Mawr beats off Viking attacks and unites Gwynedd, Powys and parts of South Wales, effectively ruling much of Wales.
1067	Chepstow Castle founded, the first Norman castle in Wales.
1131	Tintern Abbey founded.
1176	First documented Eisteddfod.
1194-1240	Llywelyn ap Iorwerth (the Great) rules most of Wales.
1215	King John signs Magna Carta and leads campaigns against Llywelyn ap Iorwerth.
1246-82	Llywelyn ap Gruffydd (the Last) rules much of Wales.
1267	Treaty of Montgomery. Llywelyn the Last recognises the English crown and is named Prince of Wales by Henry III.
1276-77	First War of Welsh Independence; Edward I (the 'hammer of the Scots') begins building stone castles in Wales. Ends with the Treaty of Aberconwy – Llywelyn loses most of his lands.
1282	Second War of Welsh Independence, Llywelyn the Last dies.

1284	Statute of Rhuddlan; Edward I imposes an English administrative system on Wales. English law takes over from Welsh in criminal matters.
1301	Edward II is first English heir to be given title Prince of Wales.
1400	Third War of Welsh Independence. Owain Glyndwr's revolt – he overruns Cardiff. A Welsh parliament is held in Machynlleth.
c1416	Owain Glyndwr dies.
1485	Battle of Bosworth. Welshman Harri Tewdwr defeats Richard III, and becomes Henry VII.
1536 and 1542	Acts of Union. Henry VIII binds Wales and England. English common law takes the place of Welsh.
1588	Translation of the Bible into Welsh, largely by William Morgan.
1642	Beginning of the Civil War. Wales is mainly Royalist.
1660	Restoration of the monarchy.
1743	Welsh Calvinist Methodist Church is founded.
1752	The Gregorian Calendar is accepted in most of Britain: the Gwaun Valley in Pembrokeshire sticks with the Julian version.
1759	Foundation of the Dowlais Ironworks and beginning of the Merthyr Tydfil iron industry. People move to the Valleys seeking work.
1793-94	Cardiff to Merthyr Canal built. Cardiff begins to grow.

1797	French troops land at Fishguard and are beaten by local militia, including local women wielding pitchforks. The last invasion on British soil.
1831	Merthyr Riots take place against appalling working conditions. The Red Flag is raised for the first time.
1839	The Chartist uprising starts – and is suppressed – in Newport.
1839-43	The Rebecca Riots, a protest against customs tariffs. Men dressed as women attack tolbooths on turnpike roads.
1847	The 'Treachery of the Blue Books' – a report condemning education in Wales – is published. Low standards blamed on the speaking of Welsh.
1858	First National Eisteddfod held in Llangollen.
1865	A Welsh colony is founded in Patagonia by Michael D Jones.
1870	Free primary schools introduced into Wales, and the speaking of Welsh is banned.
1893	University of Wales established.
1900	The Scotsman Keir Hardie is elected MP for Merthyr Tydfil – Britain's first Labour MP.
1905	Cardiff is given city status by Edward VII.
1907	Founding of the National Museum of Wales in Cardiff.
1916	David Lloyd George becomes Prime Minister.

1922	Cardiff's boundaries extended to include Llandaff and its cathedral.
1925	Plaid Cymru, the Welsh National Party, is formed.
1926	The General Strike, followed by the Great Depression (1929-34); mass unemployment hits the Valleys.
1936	Saunders Lewis and others make an arson attack on an RAF building in the Llyn, North Wales.
1948	Aneurin Bevan founds the National Health Service.
1955	Cardiff is declared capital of Wales.
1963	Welsh Language Society founded.
1979	Referendum is held on a Welsh Assembly. Eighty per cent of people say no.
1982	S4C, the Welsh language TV channel, begins broadcasting.
1984-85	Miners Strike. The Thatcher government defeats the miners and effectively finishes the industry in Wales.
1992	Welsh language Bill – Welsh is given equal status with English.
1997	Referendum on Welsh Assembly. 49.7 say no, 50.3 say yes. The tiny majority is enough to give the Assembly the go ahead.
1999	First elections to the Welsh Assembly. It starts sitting in Cardiff.
2003	Construction of new Assembly starts in Cardiff Bay.

Art and architecture

1091/1093	The Norman William Fitzhamon builds a primitive fortress in Cardiff on top of the old Roman structure.
1158	The fort at Cardiff is stormed by Ifor Bach, a local Welsh ruler. A town builds up around the castle.
1794	Following the construction of the Merthyr to Cardiff Canal, Cardiff begins to grow as coal is transported from the Valleys for trading.
1839	The second Marquess of Bute opens West Bute Dock, the first dock in Cardiff. It allows coal to be exported.
1840-64	The arrival of the railway means that Cardiff grows. Trains full of coal come to the docks from the Valleys.
1886	The Cardiff Coal Exchange is built. It cost over £40,000 and was the commercial hub of the trade with coal, cargoes and shipping space being traded.
1905	City Hall at Cathays Park is opened, an imposing building symbolic of the wealth of the coal trade.
1939-45	Cardiff's Docks are badly damaged during WW2.
1960s	Containerisation brings the docklands trade to an end. Cardiff's docks begin to disappear.
1980s	Redevelopment of the city centre takes place with the building of the St David's Centre.
1999	The Millennium Stadium is opened. The marina at Cardiff Bay is created leading to redevelopment.
2003	Construction of the new Welsh Assembly building begins.

Books

Cardiff does not feature in literature to the same extent as other UK cities like London and Edinburgh. This must partly be attributed to the city's relative youth – the early travel writers gave it only a line or two, as it scarcely merited more. That's gradually changing as the city finds its feet. In the past Welsh literature has focused more on poetry than novels, but that is beginning to change too. The suggestions below are English-language Welsh books and cover books set all over Wales.

Fiction

Brito, Leonora, *Dat's Love*. (1995), Seren Books. Story of the ethnic community in Cardiff Bay.

Cordell, Alexander, *Rape of the Fair Country* (2000), *Song of the Earth* (1999), *Hosts of Rebecca* (1998), Blorenge. This popular trilogy is set in the area around the Blaenavon ironworks during the time leading up to the Rebecca Riots.

Evans, Richard John, *Entertainment*. (2000), Seren. Lively account of living in the Rhonnda Valley.

Gower, Iris, *Copper Kingdom* (1984), *Black Gold* (1989), Arrow. Two of a number of books written by one of Wales' best-known romantic novelists.

Griffiths, Niall, *Sheepshagger* (2002), *Grits* (2001), *Kelly + Victor* (2002), *Stump* (2004), Vintage. A sort of Welsh Irvine Welsh, dealing with drugs and the seamy side of life in Wales.

Hawes, James, *White Powder, Green Light*. (2003), Jonathan Cape. A sly look at the media industry in Wales.

Llewellyn, Richard, *How Green Was My Valley*. (2001), Penguin. Probably the best known of all books about life in the Valleys.

Pryce, Malcolm, *Aberystwyth Mon Amour*. (2002), Bloomsbury. Black comedy set in contemporary Aberystwyth.

Jones, Dave and **Rivers**, Tony, *The Soul Crew*. (2002), Milo books. Looking at the sub-culture of football hooligans who follow Cardiff FC – written by one of them.

Travel writing

Abley, Mark, *Spoken Here* (2004), Heinemann. Account of the author's travels in countries that have threatened languages – or ones that are fighting back. Includes a chapter on Wales.

Borrow, George, *Wild Wales*. (1955), Gomer Press. Classic account of a 19th-century walking tour of Wales by pompous, Welsh-speaking Englishman.

Morris, Jan, *Wales*. (2000), Penguin. Rich and informative insight into the country written by Anglo-Welsh travel writer.

Morton, HV, *In Search of Wales*. (1986), Methuen. Written when the scholarly author travelled Wales in the 1930s.

Sager, Peter, *Wales*. (2002), Pallas. Extremely readable account of the country, its history and its culture.

Poetry

Thomas, Dylan, *The Dylan Thomas Omnibus*. (1999), Phoenix. An accessible collection of the poet's works.

Lycett, Andrew, *Dylan Thomas a New Life*. (2004), Weidenfeld and Nicolson. A new biography of the poet.

Manley Hopkins, Gerard, *Collected Works*, Penguin. The Jesuit poet was much influenced by the landscape of Wales.

Thomas, RS, *Selected Poems*. (2000), Phoenix. Poetry of the fiery, nationalist priest.

Webb, Harri, *Collected Poems*. (1995), Gomer Press. More contemporary poetry.

A musical tradition

The epithet 'land of song' has been attached to Wales since Adam was a lad. And, true enough, the country has a powerful musical tradition. Its male voice choirs are known throughout the world, and top-flight artists such as Tom Jones and Shirley Bassey are household names. Welsh National Opera has performed in the world's foremost venues. When virtuoso Bryn Terfel appeared at the Metropolitan Opera in 1998, he made the front page of the New York Times.

But these are conventional examples of the nation's culture – there's a lot more in the musical melting pot than this. Wales has an eclectic attitude to music, revelling in its multi facets. Organisations such as Cultural Concerns bring musicians from around the globe – Burundi, Iran, Zimbabwe, India, Poland, Colombia – to perform in Wales. Likewise, Welsh artists take the opportunity to explore cultural differences, and indeed similarities, in far flung corners of the globe.

And as for rock and pop, Wales produced The Manic Street Preachers, Stereophonics, Catatonia, Feeder, Super Furry Animals and Gorky's Zygotic Mynci, a pretty illustrious track record if ever there was one.

But why Wales and song? Why do the lusty voices of the rugby crowd belt out 'Calon Lân' and 'Sosban Fach' while the match is in full flood? What drives thousands of people to a free concert given by Welsh National Opera in Cardiff Bay? Why do pubs throughout the land reverberate to the sound, not only of the jukebox, but of imbibers boisterously accompanying their favourite number? And this isn't just drunken crooning, it actually sounds melodic!

Music, and song, is, and always has been, a compelling form of self-expression. Furthermore, Celtic societies, be they Breton, Cornish, Irish, Scottish or Welsh, have always cherished music. Music affirms an individual's sense of place and belonging.

Traditional Welsh music explores the universal themes of love and desire, but it also explores the condition of hiraeth. No single word sums up this emotion, a sense of loss and longing and nostalgia. Expats express a sense of 'hiraeth' when they think of home. But hiraeth is more than homesickness, it's part of the human condition, an inexpressible yearning. Inexpressible, that is, other than through music and song. Although the Welsh do a fine line in poetry and prose, the voice of the nation is most eloquently and profoundly expressed through the medium of music.

The earliest recorded instrument in Wales is the crwth, or lyre – there's evidence to suggest that it was played as far back as Roman times. This rudimentary instrument wasn't peculiar to the Celts though. An illustration on an Egyptian tomb circa 1900 BC shows a musician holding a six-stringed instrument that is, to all intents and purposes, a crwth.

Its heyday came in the Middle Ages when players made a good living entertaining the Welsh aristocracy. To play for the delectation of the nobles demanded years of apprenticeship and a thorough knowledge of some two dozen complex pieces. The advent of the fiddle, with its infinitely more dexterous repertoire, brought about the crwth's decline, and by the beginning of the 19th century it had been painted out of the picture.

Now, originals can be found at the Museum of Welsh Life in St Fagans near Cardiff and in the National Library of Wales in Aberystwyth. But, like many ancient art forms, the age of the crwth isn't completely over. Enthusiasts, such as widely acclaimed fiddle player Cass Meurig, still perform traditional crwth music to a small but ardent audience. Replicas are lovingly fashioned by Cardiff-based craftsman, Guy Flockhart.

Bagpipes may be synonymous with Scotland, but all Celtic nations have their own version, including this one. The Welsh manifestation is called the 'piba cwd'. Popular until the latter half of the nineteenth century, it is extraordinary that no examples have survived to the present day. Another popular instrument was the pibgorn, literally hornpipe, and by no means unique to Wales. This simple instrument is powered by a single reed like the drone reed of a bagpipe.

The triple harp, with its sweetly lyrical sound, is another instrument closely aligned with Wales. Unlike the crwth it has a prominent place in today's culture. Prince Charles recently revived an ancient tradition when he appointed 20-year-old Catrin Finch as Royal Harpist.

The young Welshwoman's mission is to bring the harp to the masses. With her youth and her perky good looks, she has a better chance of success than most of making the harp hip.

The Welsh male voice choir (cor meibion) is something of an institution. Although male choirs are found throughout the nation, they are perhaps most closely associated with the mining communities in South Wales. The demise of the coal industry isn't reflected in the fate of the choirs, and though joining one might not be a funky move, the tradition still holds firm.

Classical music enjoys a high profile in Wales. Cardiff hosts the acclaimed Singer of the World competition, attended by the great and the good among classical vocalists, on an annual basis. Welsh National Opera (WNO) is recognised as one of the UK's finest companies, and was the first ever regional company to appear at

Covent Garden. The performing arts are devotedly nurtured at the Welsh College of Music and Drama and within the BBC's National Orchestra of Wales.

The Manic Street Preachers & co paved the way for Wales to become a feature on the rock'n'roll map. Catatonia's Cerys Matthews, raunchy and vivid, sang the immortal words "Everyday I wake up, and thank the lord I'm Welsh." For a brief and wonderful moment, the South Wales city of Newport was hailed as the new Seattle. Talent scouts made a beeline for TJ's, a no bull venue famed for spawning raw young talent.

For those jaded with the 'We'll Keep A Welcome in the Hillsides' image of Wales, this feisty new face represented a freedom from the shackles of tradition. For the first time ever it was cool to be Welsh. The term 'Cool Cymru' or 'Cool Wales' entered the lexicon.

Rhondda, the most famous of all the South Wales mining valleys, struck out into new waters with a musical venture called The Pop Factory. This sleek venue and TV complex operates from the old fizzy drinks factory (remember Dandelion & Burdock?). It has worked hard to attract big names, with notable success. Hot shots like Travis, Sophie Ellis-Bextor, Lost Prophets and Victoria Beckham have all graced its stage, while bands like Blue and Mis-Teeq had their first outing here.

Although the Manics and the Stereophonics remain in the major league, and Cerys Matthews is forging ahead with a solo career of considerable depth, some would say that the contemporary music scene has stalled, at least, in terms of bands big enough to hit the headlines and stay there.

All is not lost though. The Welsh Music Foundation has been set up to nurture modern Welsh music, and maximise its cultural and economic potential. Sadly, to date, the mother country has benefited very little in monetary terms from the success of its high-flying sons and daughters. In future that should change, and Wales can reap financial and emotional rewards from her aeons-long love affair with music.

Language

Welsh is an Indo-European language, presumably descended like most (but not all) languages in modern Western Europe from languages that were originally spoken on the steppes of Central Asia. It is one of the oldest European languages and immediately descended from the Brythonic language; its closest relatives are the other Celtic languages – Cornish and Breton. To the present day there remain differences in dialects throughout Wales, the most notable being between: Y Wyndodeg (northwest), Y Buwyseg (northeast and mid Wales), Y Ddyfydeg (southwest), Gwenhwyseg (southeast).

Wales is officially bilingual and welsh is now spoken by almost a quarter of the population. A visitor is sure to see unusual phrases and hear unfamiliar sounds, but this is part of Wales' charm. Try and get your tongue around some basic welsh and you'll receive a warm welcome wherever you go.

Alphabet (Yr Wyddor)
a, b, c, ch, d, dd, e, f, ff, g, ng, h, i, i, l, ll, m, n, o, p, ph, r, rh, s, t, th, u, w, y

Vowels (llafariad)
a, e, i, o, u, w, y

A	aah	NG	eng	PH	phee
B	bee	H	high-tsh	R	air
C	eck	I	ee	RH	air-hee
CH	ech	J	jay	S	ess
D	dee	L	el	T	tee
DD	edd	LL	ell	TH	eth
E	air	M	em	U	ee
F	ev	N	en	W	oo
FF	eff	O	oh	Y	uh
G	egg	P	pee		

Welsh place names

Welsh	Meaning	Pronunciation
Abertawe (Swansea)	Estuary	Ab-er-taw-eh
Beddgelert	Grave	Be-the-gel-airt
Betws-y-Coed	Wood	Bet-oos uh koyd
Caerdydd (Cardiff)	Fort	K-ie-r-dee-the
Casnewydd (Newport)	New	Kas ne with
Dinbych-y-Pysgod (Denbigh)	Fish	Din-bich uh pusg-od
Eryri (Snowdonia)	Eagle	Err ur ee
Glan Llyn	Lake	Glan ll-in
Llandeilo	Church	ll-an-day-lo
Pwllheli	Pool	Pw-ll-el-ee
Sir Benfro (Pembrokeshire)	County	Seer Ben Vr-aw
Y Drenewydd (Newtown)	Town	Uh Drair ne with
Ynys Mon (Anglesey)	Island	Un- is Morn

Llanfairpwllgwyngyllgogerychwyrndrobwllllantysiliogogogoch
Roughly translated as:

The Church of St. Mary by the pool with the white hazel near the rapid whirlpool by St. Tysilio's church and the red cave.

Have a go at pronouncing it:
Thlann vyre pooth gwin gith gogger ich chweern drobbooth lann tuss-illyo goggo gauch.

Some useful phrases:

English	Welsh	Rough pronunciation
Thank you very much	*Diolch yn Fawr*	Dee-och unn vowr
Goodbye	*Hwyl*	Who-ill
Good morning	*Bore da*	Bor-air daah

Index

Check out...

WWW...

100 travel guides, 100s of destinations, 5 continents
and 1 Footprint...

www.footprintbooks.com

Credits

Footprint credits

Text editor: Alan Murphy
Assistant editor: Laura Dixon
Map editor: Sarah Sorensen

Publisher: Patrick Dawson
Series created by Rachel Fielding
Cartography: Claire Benison, Kevin
Feeney, Robert Lunn
Proofreading: Catherine Charles

Design: Mytton Williams
Maps: Footprint Handbooks Ltd

Photography credits

Front cover: Wales on View (Whale
sculpture)
Inside: Alys Tomlinson (p1 Welsh lion, p5
Scott Memorial, p29 Cardiff Bay, p59
Tintern Abbey)
Back cover: Alys Tomlinson (Cardiff Castle)
Generic images: John Matchett

Print

Manufactured in Italy by Legoprint.
Pulp from sustainable forests.

Footprint feedback

We try as hard as we can to make
each Footprint guide as up to date
as possible, but, of course, things
always change. If you want to let us
know about your experiences – good,
bad or ugly – then don't delay, go to
www.footprintbooks.com and send
in your comments.
® Footprint Handbooks and the Footprint
mark are a registered trademark of
Footprint Handbooks Ltd

Publishing information

Footprint Cardiff
1st edition
Text and maps © Footprint Handbooks
Ltd July 2004

ISBN 1 904777 05 8
CIP DATA: a catalogue record for this
book is available from the British Library

Published by Footprint
6 Riverside Court
Lower Bristol Road
Bath, BA2 3DZ, UK
T +44 (0)1225 469141
F +44 (0)1225 469461
E discover@footprintbooks.com
W www.footprintbooks.com

Distributed in the USA by
Publishers Group West

Publishing stuff

Complete title list

(P) denotes pocket
Handbook

For a different view…
choose a Footprint

Over 100 Footprint travel guides
Covering 150 of the world's most exciting countries and cities
in Latin America, the Caribbean, Africa, Indian sub-continent,
Australasia, North America, Southeast Asia, the Middle East
and Europe.

Discover so much more…
The finest writers. In-depth knowledge. Entertaining and accessible.
Critical restaurant and hotels reviews. Lively descriptions of all the
attractions. Get away from the crowds.

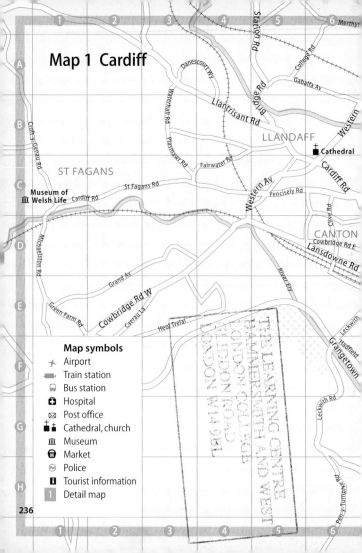

Map 1 Cardiff

Map symbols

- ✈ Airport
- 🚆 Train station
- 🚌 Bus station
- ✛ Hospital
- ✉ Post office
- ✝✝ Cathedral, church
- 🏛 Museum
- 🎪 Market
- Ⓟ Police
- ℹ Tourist information
- ① Detail map

LLANDAFF

✝ Cathedral

ST FAGANS

🏛 Museum of Welsh Life

CANTON

Station Rd
Merthyr
Danescourt Wy
College Rd
Gabalfa Av
Bridge Rd
Western
Llantrisant Rd
Waterhall Rd
Plasmawr Rd
Fairwater Rd
Cardiff Rd
Western Av
Pencisely Rd
Clive Rd
St Fagans Rd
Coed-y-Gaeau Rd
Cowbridge Rd E
Cardiff Rd
Cowbridge Rd E
Lansdowne Rd
Michaelston Rd
Grand Av
River Ely
Green Farm Rd
Cowbridge Rd W
Caerau La
Heol Trelai
Leckwith
Hadfield
Grangetown
Leckwith Rd
Penny-Tumpike Rd

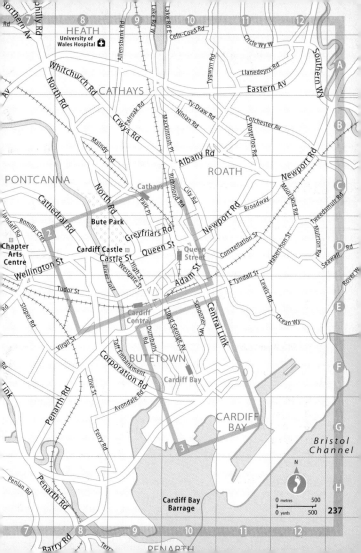

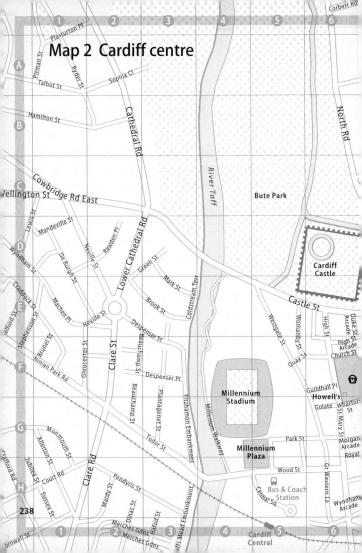

Map 2 Cardiff centre

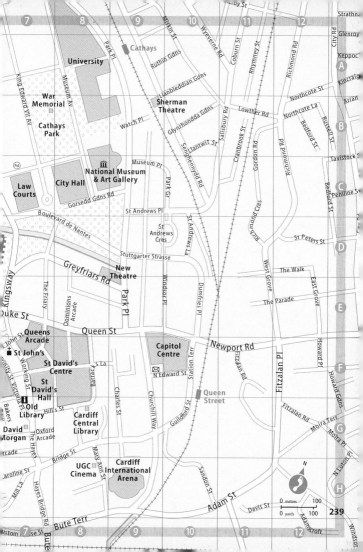

Map 3 Cardiff Bay

240